Changing Cadence

Meditations on Life, Family and Country from a

Leather Bicycle Seat

Michael A. Dillon

Oosik Publishing
Changing Cadence—Meditations on Life, Family and Country
from a Leather Bicycle Seat
Michael Dillon

Cover Design: Kevin Story

ISBN: 0986057703
ISBN 13: 9780986057700
Published in the United States by Oosik Publishing

For Liz
(aka "W.C.C.")

Contents

Section 4

Section 5

Changing Cadence

Preface

"There's only two things in life.
- But, I forget what they are."
John Hiatt, *Buffalo River Home*[1]

I looked out over the blanket of clouds below as the plane headed east. An occasional seam opened in the whiteness revealing a web of isolated roads and remote towns. Leaning my head against the window, I wondered about the people of these small communities—who they were; what they did; how they raised their children; how they lived. It was something that I had thought about before.

I grew up the son of a Naval aviator. Along with my mother and two brothers, we moved around the United States in a path well-worn by other military families, relocating from Pensacola, Florida, to Coronado, California, to Brunswick, Georgia, to Whidbey Island, Washington, among other places. It happened almost every year of my youth. Our father would announce that he had a new deployment, and almost as a reflex, the family would start loading cardboard boxes into a green and yellow Mayflower moving van. Then we would pile into our car and drive thousands of miles to our next new home.

For me, many of those miles were spent in the backward-facing seat in the rear of our Chrysler Town and Country station wagon. Although the term "time out" was not yet part of the parental vernacular, that's where we sat when we were being punished. On most trips, it seemed that I was the accused instigator of inter-vehicular battles with my two younger brothers. Consequently, I travelled thousands of miles looking through that lonely rear window.

My brothers and I hated that spot. It was the automotive equivalent of a Siberian gulag. Isolated from the rest of the family, we watched the world

---

[1] John Hiatt is a musical god. There, I've said it.

pass by through a dusty glass window that magnified the sunlight and heated the light brown vinyl upholstery. It made us feel sluggish and sick. But that perspective gave me more time to consider what I saw on the road as it slowly disappeared into a point in the distance.

As we travelled the empty stretches of asphalt, I would look at the people of the small hamlets, farms and ranches still in my line of vision. I would wonder: Who lives there? What is their history? How are they different from the people I know?

And then I'd usually get carsick and barf.

Many years later, I had the opportunity to answer some of these questions when Sun Microsystems, the company where I worked, was acquired and I was out of a job. I could write volumes about Sun: its long history of innovation, unique corporate culture and wonderful people. I had worked there for almost 15 years, but I was still excited to go to the office every day. Our chairman exemplified the place. When asked in an employee meeting whether Sun had a dress code, he replied, "Yes, please dress." He rallied employees by always ending speeches with "Kick butt and have fun." Some of my most enriching career experiences occurred there, and it was a source of many long-term friendships. Sun was the most special of companies, and seeing it sold was emotionally wrenching.

As the company's chief legal officer, I was intensely involved in the sale of the company to Oracle Corporation. Over a period of 18 months, we negotiated merger agreements, responded to countless requests for corporate information and planned for the integration of the two companies. Along the way we also navigated almost every legal hurdle that one could face in a large corporate acquisition, including battling antitrust challenges, dealing with market rumors, and responding to stockholder litigation. It often seemed that this exhausting acquisition process would never end. I know it felt that way to those who worked for me. I could see the fatigue and uncertainty in their eyes. Almost every day I would find myself meeting with employees and trying to help them remain confident and plan for the future in the face of overwhelming concerns about losing their jobs in the midst of one of the nation's most severe economic recessions.

Working weekends and late nights, I watched as my weight and blood pressure rose and my ability to sleep disappeared. In the midst of the stress and strain of providing professional and emotional support for stockholders, employees, executives, and our board of directors during this turbulent time, I sought a diversion—something I could look forward to when the work was done. In the recesses of my mind, an idea slowly took hold: What if I took a long bike ride? Alone. Across the United States.

I still don't know the precise origin of the thought. I had been a weekend cyclist for years, but had never done any serious bicycle touring. I was one of those guys you see on a Saturday morning with a shiny bicycle and a cycling jersey that looks much too tight, like a human sausage casing. I would like to say that I was supremely confident in my ability to pedal across the country, but that would be disingenuous. I had never ventured an undertaking like this before. But, it wasn't the goal of crossing the country that motivated me. Instead, it was the idea of a journey. After more than 25 years of giving all my energy to my family and career, I knew that I was exhausted and needed to change the pace of my life, to find some time for introspection and exploration. I hoped that this ride would provide that opportunity and, along the way, some answers to the questions asked by that young boy looking out of the back of the station wagon so many years earlier.

Gradually and quietly, I began sharing my plans with others. To be honest, "plans" is probably a bit of a stretch. I've always prioritized action over logistics, and friends and family have tried to deal with this often-frustrating character trait. For example, years ago I purchased a collapsible two-person kayak and, on a whim, persuaded a friend who lived in Southern California to go for a "little outing." The idea was that I would drive down from my home near San Francisco, pick him up, and we'd paddle the 33 miles from Laguna Beach to Catalina Island, camp overnight, and then paddle back the following day.

My friend quickly vetoed the plan and insisted that we take the ferry to Catalina and paddle back to the coast of California, saying: "Mike, I have no faith in your ability to navigate to an island, but I'm certain that not even you could miss an entire continent." It was this same friend who also remembered a few other things that I had never thought to include for our little outing, like sunscreen, a compass, and glow sticks to illuminate the kayak in the early morning darkness of the busy shipping lanes we were crossing. Most importantly, he thought to bring along a specially marked "pee" bottle, which came to good use many times during the more than 10 hours of paddling in choppy seas.

Now, when I raised the idea of my cycling odyssey to those close to me, I met a fair bit of resistance. A number of people challenged my age (just north of 50), conditioning (excellent, if the activity was raising a cold beer), and, above all else, my mental stability (always questionable to begin with). For some friends, it was just another of my ideas that they believed would end only as talk.

The only exception was my immediate family. My wife, Liz, and I had been married for almost 25 years. She and our three teenaged children—Declan, Emily, and Bryce—had become accustomed to my wanderlust, which to their dismay often included adventurous locations for family holidays, but on a shoe-string budget and with little planning on my part. A family vacation in Prague included a stay in a hotel where we had to step over a drunk to get into our room; a Christmas holiday trip exploring Australia was spent in a motorhome that broke down two days into the trip; our camping trip in New Mexico was scheduled for July (I forgot about the 105 degree heat); and the flat I rented in Paris off the Internet ended up being located in a rather dodgy area in a red light district. So, when I raised my plan of doing a ride across the country, camping and staying in low budget motels, I was confident of my family's support and certain that they would not want to join me.

As my company's acquisition was nearing a close, I floated a trial balloon past Liz late one evening when I arrived home from work.

"Hi, honey. How was the day?" she asked, while stirring something on the stove.

"A tough one. I had another person in my office today who broke down and started crying because she's worried about losing her job. It's very depressing. At least the acquisition should be final soon, and this will all be over."

"Then what? Have you thought about it?"

"Liz, I need a break. I'm burnt-out."

"I know. We all see it. We're just trying to let you have some space. What about a vacation?"

"Well," I said, spotting my opening, "I was thinking about that, but the kids are still in school, and their summer break is five months away. I think I need something more immediate. Perhaps, I should just do something on my own", I said as though the thought had just occurred to me.

"Like what? For how long?" She continued to stir.

"I'm not really sure. But one wild idea I had was to ride my bicycle across the country. I've wanted to explore more of America since I was a kid and this might be an interesting way to do it."

I held my breath. Seconds passed.

"Sounds like fun," she said, finally. "Would you hand me that bowl, please?"

Wow, that was easy, I thought. For a moment I considered that Liz might secretly desire to get me out of the house so that she could have a liaison with a pool boy or gardener, but as we had neither, I decided that she just must be supportive.

Next, I approached the kids. As every college student remembers, the "Planck unit" is the shortest known unit of time as measured by the speed of light travelling through a vacuum. It was also an approximate measurement of my teenagers' attention span when I distracted them from their electronic devices and social networking sites to tell them of my plan. Catching them on the couch watching television one evening, I raised the idea.

"Hi Dad," said Declan. "How was work?"

"Exhausting, but it's almost done—the sale of the company will be over soon."

"Really?" said Emily, looking up from her phone. "What happens then?"

"Well, I've got to look for a new job."

"You mean we won't have any money?" asked Bryce with alarm.

"No, no. We're fine. Your mom and I have done a good job of saving."

"That's good," he replied with obvious relief.

"But I may take some time off before I begin looking. I'm not sure I'm ready to jump back into a new job."

"What would you do if you weren't working?" asked Emily (which I immediately interpreted as: "Please, please don't stay at home all day giving us 'projects'.").

"Well, one idea I had was to do something different, like ride my bicycle across the country."

Their response was immediate, energetic, and imploring: "We don't have to go, do we?!"

I reassured them that I would not take them out of school and that this would not be a family vacation. With relief written on their faces, they returned to their electronics, giving me little more than a "That's cool. Have fun, Dad."

When I began telling other family members about my trip the reaction was far different and I struggled to remain confident and composed.

"You'll never do it," said my brother Kevin. "You're not that stupid. You'll get killed."

My cousin Mike warned, "I used to work in the South. Those people are different—and dangerous. Especially out in the bayous. You can't do it by yourself."

"That would be the most fuckin' irresponsible thing you've ever done!" exclaimed my father in his booming military officer voice as he jabbed a finger at my chest. Most irresponsible? Really? As he spoke, a "Mike's Greatest Hits" of youthful transgressions ran through my mind. For example, I really did wipe poison oak on the pillow and sheets of my brother's bed when we were teenagers. But at this stage of life, and understanding what it's like to be a father, I realized that he was speaking from fear for someone he loved. So I put a hand on his shoulder and said in a reassuring voice, "I'll be OK, Dad. Really."

But a part of me wondered if I would.

Shaking away the uncertainty, I tried to focus on basic preparations. While I was certain that I could figure out most things as I travelled, I knew that I needed a dependable touring bicycle and one that fit me well. Touring bikes are different than their road bike cousins. They generally have a longer wheelbase and wider tires to provide more comfort. They also have stronger frames and a better range of gearing to handle the weight of the additional equipment and supplies of a touring cyclist. It's like the difference between driving your father's Lincoln Town Car and your brother's Porsche 911. After some research, I found a shop operated by Bruce Gordon in Petaluma, California, that had a reputation for building solid custom touring bikes, and I drove up for a visit.

Gordon's shop brought to mind Dr. Emmett Brown's laboratory from the movie *Back to the Future*. It was strewn with bicycle frames, wheels, and parts. There were also tools, broken furniture, an old motorcycle, stacks of papers—and amongst it all, some of the most beautiful handmade bicycles I had ever seen. They were two-wheeled works of art worthy of display in the MoMA.

While Mr. Gordon obviously deserved his reputation for craftsmanship, his customer service was lacking. I walked around his small shop looking at the bicycles while he typed away at an ancient computer behind a desk piled high with decades of old catalogs and magazines without taking notice of me.

Finally, I cleared my throat and asked him if he could answer some questions about his touring bicycles. His terse response conveyed that he felt that he was doing me a favor, but he appeared to warm up once he understood that I was interested in making a purchase. After he provided information about the composition and geometry of the frame he discussed the components that were available. The bike he showed me had shifters on the ends of the handlebars.

"On my bike at home the shifters are integrated into the brake levers," I said. "Can I get the same thing on this bike?"

"No," he said with a look of distain.

"I'm happy paying a bit extra for that feature if price is an issue."

"No."

"I'm not sure I understand. Why can't I order a different type of shifter?"

"Because I've been making these damn bikes for more than 30 years and I know what's best!" he exclaimed angrily.

You don't often find someone so confident in his craft that he feels comfortable risking a sale by being short-tempered with a customer. I decided to trust his judgment and made the decision on the spot to order a touring bike built to my measurements. It was a decision I would never regret and the bicycle he built for me became my close companion.

A few days later, I bought a set of front and rear panniers (large black saddlebags for my gear). I wanted to travel as light as possible, so I decided to bring only my sleeping bag and air mattress, a bivouac (bivy) sack for protection at night, a stove (minus a fuel canister that I'd need to find en route), and a single pot for cooking—leaving behind my tent, additional cooking gear, lantern, and warm winter clothing. My electronics included a laptop, camera, iPod, cell phone, GPS, and far too many electrical cords. I also brought along clothes, a few days' worth of freeze-dried food, three water bottles, toiletries, maps, books, repair equipment...and at least a touch of growing anxiety.

Given that it was late January, the season dictated my choice of route, so I purchased a set of maps from Adventure Cycling Association, an excellent non-profit organization providing support for touring cyclists, which traced a path across the southern portion of the country. The maps covered a narrowly defined area, but I decided that I would supplement them with other maps that I would buy along the way. Worst case, I'd just point my bike in a direction, pedal and figure it out as I traveled.

But which direction? It's a source of great debate among cyclists. I knew that the forceful winds of the jet stream move in an easterly direction, which would suggest that travelling with them at my back would make for a more efficient and enjoyable ride. On the other hand, ground level wind conditions vary with topographical features and can result in a tailwind even when heading west.

Ultimately, I made the decision to ride east to west. I felt that heading home to my family would motivate me when the pedaling was at its most challenging. And, after all, how bad could the wind be?

In the end of January, the acquisition of my company was finalized, and my position was eliminated. I came into work one morning, packed my boxes, turned in my badge to the human resources representative, and signed my termination documents. Even though it was expected, it felt sudden, like the deceleration one feels when a roller coaster comes to rest. After years focused on work and career, now all that came to mind was uncertainty. What was I going to do with the rest of my life? Given the slow economic conditions, could I really afford to take time off to make this ride—or should I be looking for a job? Was my father correct? Was this an irresponsible, selfish thing to do? Would I fall victim to some accident or crime? What if I didn't make it across the country? Would I be embarrassed by my failure?

A few weeks later, I found myself flying to Florida to start my journey and to try to find the answers to these questions. Leaning away from the window of the plane, I used a pen and some drink coasters to calculate what I would be facing. According to my calculations, for each hour of the six-hour flight to Florida from my home in California, I would be riding 10 to 12 days on my return. The thought was staggering, especially given that it took several beers for me to obtain the requisite number of coasters for this exacting computation.

I spent the rest of the flight gazing out the window in a haze of hops and barley, distracted by thoughts of bike, gear, and route logistics. Surprisingly absent from my mind, given what I would face in the weeks ahead, was the thought: "What in the hell am I doing?"

Section 1

Whereupon Our Hero Faces Adverse Weather Conditions
and Develops an Unnatural Affection for
Desitin Diaper Rash Ointment.

(Florida and Alabama)

one

Jacksonville to Lake City, Florida
Total Ride Mileage: 86

I awoke early and looked out the window of my second story motel room and to the beach east of Jacksonville, Florida. Before me was the Atlantic Ocean and an unbroken expanse of heavy gray clouds. For a few moments I sat on the edge of the bed looking at the inclement weather. I wondered whether I was really ready for this. Choosing motion over further self-doubt, I arose, took a quick shower, quietly assembled my bicycle and racks, and loaded my panniers. Despite the care I had taken to pack light, my bicycle and gear weighed over 100 pounds on the bathroom scale. Adding my body weight meant that I would be moving more than 300 lbs. (or, in beer weight—one of my favorite units of measure—about eight cases of bottled beer) across the country using only my own power.

Donning my rain gear, I wheeled my bicycle out of the hotel and headed to the beach for the perfunctory "start of the journey" photograph. Given the cold wind and foreboding skies, I couldn't find anyone nearby to take my picture until a bearded, apparently homeless man rolled up on a rusted beach cruiser with several trash bags of possessions hanging from his handlebars. "Excuse me," I said. "I'm starting a ride across the country and wondered if you would take a picture of me before I get going."

He looked slowly at my heavily loaded bicycle and then at me as I handed him the camera. Still silent, he took my picture and returned the camera. When he finally started to speak, I braced myself for a plea for money. Instead, he gave me a "soul shake" with a heavily calloused hand and in a low, gravelly voice said: "Real cool, man. Be safe."

With that, I headed off, experiencing a mixture of excitement and apprehension, heightened by the gloomy weather and unexpectedly cold temperature.

One of my goals for the trip was to lose the extra weight gained from all of those years sitting behind a desk. To this end, I adamantly resolved that I would not eat at any fast-food restaurants for the length of my ride. That pledge lasted exactly the 6.7 miles it took me to ride to a Chick-fil-A restaurant for breakfast and a break from the cold weather.

I sat down in a red padded booth and studied the menu above the counter looking for something to help me get warm. A very overweight clerk who was busing tables nearby noticed my riding attire, and in a stream of Southern drawl said: "Y'all gettin' some exercise? After work I'm doin' that too, for my diabetes. And, ya know what? It turns out exercise is good for all kinds of other things like yur heart, yur lungs, yur legs, and yur weight."

Perhaps it was the inclement weather and the long day ahead of me, but my inner, more sarcastic voice wanted to say: "Wow! Who knew? We should get the word out on this." But instead, I just smiled and nodded.

After finishing my meal, I left the restaurant under dark clouds that quickly gave way to heavy rain, making for a cold, wet ride into Jacksonville. At one point, I resorted to huddling under an overpass for more than half an hour, slapping my hands on my shoulders and running in place in an attempt to stay warm and dry while waiting out the rain.

My God, I thought, this is Florida, the "Sunshine State", and the weather is this bad?

When the storm at last decreased to a mere downpour, I rode over the Isaiah D. Hart Bridge and into Jacksonville city. The bridge scared the hell out of me. It was a long arching expanse rising high over the St. John River. As it had no bicycle lane or sidewalk, I was forced to ride on a shoulder that was less than 12 inches wide. With cars in such close proximity I was repeatedly sprayed with sheets of filthy muck by each passing vehicle. To add to the excitement, several sections of the bridge were joined with metal plates with openings that looked like the gaping maw of some bicycle-rim-eating monster.

But I made it across, and by mid-afternoon I had navigated around the periphery of urban Jacksonville and was moving through a more rural setting toward Osceola National Forest, where I had originally planned to camp for the evening. It was only my first day, and I was wet, cold, and miserable. Although I had covered more than 40 miles, the adverse conditions provided my first real insight into what I had before me. How was I ever going to do this for 3,450 more miles?

To make matters worse, I hadn't been able to find a fuel canister that fit my stove at any stores that I had passed during the day. Without one, I wouldn't be able to heat my freeze-dried food, so a Snickers candy bar would have to serve as that evening's repast. My only other choice was to continue to ride to the next major town, Lake City, and hope that it had a motel and a place for a warm meal.

As I pedaled, I debated what to do, until, with the sun setting and my fatigue rising, I pulled to the side of the road and used my cell phone to call Liz, or "W.C.C." (Wife Command Center) as I affectionately referred to her. As I dialed her number, my body began shaking from the chill. I was aching and drenched, and my legs were caked in mud and grime from the wet roadways and passing cars. I had barely started my journey, and I was already at a low point.

After a few rings, Liz answered the phone in a hurried voice: "Hello?"

"Hi, honey. It's Mike."

"How are you? Is everything OK?" she asked anxiously. "I'm just leaving to take Bryce to his friend's house. He's waiting in the car."

"Yes, I'm fine. I just need to know if a town called Lake City, Florida, has any motels. I may change my plans about camping tonight."

After a quick bit of typing on the computer she returned to the phone and confirmed that Lake City had a number of motels. Then she said: "Mike, I want to talk more, but Bryce is in the car. I've really got to go." In hindsight, it was a blessing that she was pressed for time, because a longer, more sympathetic conversation would likely have resulted in me uttering the words: "I WANT TO COME HOME!" Instead, I gave her a quick goodbye, zipped my rain jacket, and climbed back on my bike.

While I pedaled the few remaining hours through the rain toward lodging in Lake City, the great British adventurer Wilfred Thesiger (best known for his trek through the Empty Quarter of Arabia) came to mind. More than a decade ago, he was asked his thoughts about another explorer who was then traversing

Africa's dangerous Congo basin. Thesiger commented that while the activity was interesting, it couldn't truly be called an "adventure" because the explorer possessed a satellite phone and could raise help whenever needed.

As someone who had enjoyed many evenings lying in a sleeping bag, looking up at the cosmos, I had planned this trip with the idea that I would camp almost every night, that it would be true adventure. Now, after only a day of riding, the fatigue and unexpectedly cold and wet weather caused me to reconsider my plans. And so, as I reached Lake City at the end of the day—and with all deference to Mr. Thesiger—I was quite satisfied trading adventure for a comfortable bed and a hot shower.

two

Lake City to Tallahassee, Florida
Total Ride Mileage: 206

As you are reading this, warm and relaxed in your bed or chair, dozens of people are traversing North America by bicycle. It doesn't matter the time of year. They are out there, slowly making their way across the continent. Many travel in pairs—a married couple enjoying retirement, college sweethearts escaping their studies, a couple of middle-aged buddies looking for excitement. Some travel as part of large organized groups with "sag" vehicles transporting gear and providing logistical support. Others break the ride into sections, covering a quarter of the distance each year due to limitations of time or money. Some race across the country focused only on covering the distance as quickly as possible. Some wander. Some ride for the sense of achievement, some for cocktail party bragging rights, some to forget, and some to discover.

And, some, like me, aren't quite sure why they are doing it.

After leaving Lake City the following morning, I met two sets of people riding east to the Atlantic, the first of a number of cyclists that I would encounter in the weeks ahead. One was a delightful couple in their early twenties who both worked for the U.S. Forestry Service in Missoula, Montana. They had started riding in Washington, worked their way down to Southern California, and from there across the U.S.—or, as they described it, "2,000 miles and a big left turn." Listening to the excitement in their voices as they described their experience made me wonder why I hadn't tried something like this when I was their age. Why had I been in such a hurry to pursue a career?

Less than an hour later, I encountered two scruffy men also riding east: one was a visitor from England and the other was from California. They had met as they crossed the country on their way to St. Augustine, Florida, and had decided to ride together. They had intended to complete their ride there, but were now thinking it might be interesting to continue down through South America. Here I was, anxious about heading across the U.S., and they were describing the idea of an additional 4,000 miles on another continent as an interesting "little detour."

Listening to the relaxed confidence in their voices as they shared insights on places to camp, interesting communities and historical sites provided me with a bit of much needed inspiration. Maybe this would all work out, I thought as I pedaled away.

While the day was sunny and the skies clear, the headwind was constant. Riding a bicycle on even a windless day is an energy-losing pursuit. On a flat road, aerodynamic drag accounts for more than 70% of the resistance a person feels while pedaling. High pressure builds in front of the rider and low pressure behind, in effect sucking the rider backwards. That's the reason bicycle manufacturers invest so much effort in creating gear that is not only lighter, but also more aerodynamic. Riding into a heavy wind just increases the resistance. Riding in these conditions with panniers—well, it's like pedaling a large steamer trunk.

The only interruption in my miserable windblown reverie was when a dog that looked like a pit bull-dachshund mix chased me down Country Road 132. This small but frightening mongrel came racing out of nowhere. With a throaty growl and snapping jaws, it sprinted after my wheel, throwing me into panic.

The riders I met that morning had cautioned me about dog attacks and passed on various strategies for dealing with them, including bear spray, dog biscuits, and air horns. Because of their warning, I had placed a handful of throwing-sized stones in my jersey pocket that I quickly retrieved as I stood up in my cleats and began pedaling furiously. As the dog closed the distance to within a few feet, I started to throw one but found that I couldn't bring myself to hit an animal with a rock, not even a dog as threatening as this one. Instead, I accelerated more until, after a quarter of a mile of sprinting, the dog fell behind and finally lost interest. When I last looked over my shoulder, he was standing in the middle of the road giving me a final bark, warning me never to return.

The scenery grew more appealing as I continued on in the direction of the Suwannee River, made famous in the song by Stephen Foster. Saw palmettos, long leaf pines (used for the masts of 19th century sailing ships), and red cedars lined the road. From a large oak, Spanish moss blew toward me like an airport windsock. Scattered along the horizon, kudzu-covered frames of ramshackle shotgun shacks provided a remembrance of the historical past.

In the late afternoon, I surrendered to the wind and found a place to camp at Suwannee River State Park. It was a secluded campground that was almost empty at this time of year. The surroundings were quiet and peaceful like the dark, slow-moving Suwannee River that curved through the forest on its 230-mile course to the Gulf of Mexico.

I set up my bivy sack, which is little more than a water proof shell for a sleeping bag, in a cluster of oak trees that I hoped would provide additional shelter. Then I headed off to the restroom to shower and change clothes. This campground had not only warm showers, but also a book exchange, which was a delightful discovery. On the flight to Jacksonville, I had finished my only book. Since then, I had been looking without success for a bookstore. The bad news was that the best (and I'm serious here) book available in the campground was a hardback edition of Irish dancer Michael Flatley's autobiography, *Lord of the Dance*. As tempting as that was, I left the book and, after enjoying a nice hot shower, walked to a bench overlooking the river to enjoy the setting sun and a cup of hot tea.

As I watched the muddy water quietly pass, I sought deep and powerful thoughts about my 50-plus years on the planet, life-altering thoughts—the kind of thoughts Carlos Castaneda recounted in *The Teachings of Don Juan*—except without the peyote. Unfortunately, I found that I was simply too tired even for this moment of reflection. And so, I gulped down the last of my tea and navigated through the trees in the twilight until I found my campsite, where I burrowed into my bag and fell asleep instantly.

After saddling up the next morning, I passed through the town of Lee, Florida (pop. 402). The sign at the entrance to the town boasted: "Lee, Florida—Little

But Proud." It was a placid community that consisted of little more than a few dozen well-kept homes on the side of the roadway. No commercial buildings, churches, schools, or even citizens were in sight. I rode past wondering how the people of Lee spent their days and where they all were. Later, curiosity got the best of me and I looked up the town's home page on the Internet. Under the "Events" section, it listed only a single item: "fishing."

A few miles past Lee, I pulled over when I saw a cyclist off to the side of the road standing beside his bicycle and an overloaded trailer. Sometimes you meet a stranger, say "hello," and they are instantly forgotten. At other times, like this, they are unforgettable.

The cyclist introduced himself as "Don." He was in his mid-fifties with a thin gray ponytail and a roguish, gap-toothed smile, which he displayed frequently as we compared notes on how badly our butts ached. Reaching into his cycling trailer, Don pulled out a large Tupperware container and offered me a homemade granola bar. While munching away, we stood side by side and talked with our faces turned toward the first warm sunshine in days.

Much of our discussion was about our gear. Given my exhaustion after only a few days of riding, I was convinced that I was carrying too much weight. On particularly tough stretches of hills or pushing into a strong wind, I would fantasize not about Victoria's Secret supermodels, but about abandoning some of my gear on the side of the road.

After meeting Don, I realized it could have been worse. Before starting the ride, I had considered pulling a trailer, but cycling trailers provide plenty of space, and I knew from experience that empty space always gets filled—witness my wife's side of the bedroom closet. Don confirmed my thinking. Behind him, he towed the trailer, which was piled three feet high with all manner of gear held together by straps and a heavy cable lock, topped off with an American flag flying from a small flexible pole. In addition, he had a storage bag between his handlebars and a two-person tent strapped to a rack over his rear wheel.

"How do you like pulling a trailer?" I asked.

"Well, it tracks nicely. I don't even notice it on the road, other than the weight. Are you happy with the panniers?"

"Yes," I said. "They force me to pack light. Once they're filled, you can't really carry anything else."

"I kind of get that now. After a few days on the road, I'm thinking I brought way too much stuff."

"I wondered about that. What do you have in there?" I asked, pointing to the trailer.

"Well, in this bag, I have my winter clothes. In this one, I have my riding clothes. This one is my sleeping bag, and this one is a three-person tent."

"Wait a second, you've got a tent strapped to the rear rack—you have two tents?"

"Yeah, I wasn't sure which one to use, so I brought them both."

"Okay…I noticed you also have a bear-proof food canister. Are bears a problem around here?" I asked with some trepidation.

"I don't know, but I thought, well, I have a trailer. I have room. So, what the hell, I might as well be prepared."

Good thing bike trailers come in only one size, I thought. If they offered any more room, Don would never make it.

In the course of our conversation, we realized we were following roughly the same route across the country, yet neither of us raised the possibility of riding together. In part, this was because we travelled at differing speeds. But there was also an unspoken desire within each of us to make the journey on our own. Without expressly acknowledging that we were committed to traveling alone—while at the same time feeling apprehensive about it—we exchanged phone numbers and agreed that we would keep in touch. I also forwarded Don's information to Liz so that when I went missing in some remote bayou, my family would have someone they could contact to start the search for my body.

three

Tallahassee to DeFuniak Springs, Florida
Total Ride Mileage: 347

If you were to ask my children, I think they would agree that one of my major shortcomings as a parent is my compulsion to pull over at every historical road-side marker, monument, and park. I can't restrain myself. It's a family tradition that I chalk up to my father, who subjected his three sons to the same on the many cross-country drives of our youth.

Now, I was discovering that one of the hidden pleasures of this ride was my complete freedom to stop at historical sites without hearing the protests of my three teenagers. Taking advantage of this autonomy, I altered my planned course and detoured to visit Letchworth-Love Mounds Archeological State Park, an interesting but strangely named place, which, as a friend pointed out, sounded much like the moniker of a Victorian-era porn star.

There was no one else in the park as I explored the remains of a 1,100-year-old society created by a group known as the Weeden Island natives. It consisted of several earthen mounds the size of large office buildings that were used as platforms and burial grounds for these ancient people. As I walked around, it took a bit of imagination to visualize the civilization that once existed there, but seeing the remains of the Weeden foreshadowed the transitory nature of many communities I would visit throughout my ride—communities that were declining or disappearing as the result of economic downturn due to dramatic shifts in manufacturing or commerce or from force of nature as by Hurricane Katrina.

But, good news for the kids: I took lots of pictures!

After days of quiet two-lane country roads, the highway traffic on the approach into Tallahassee was frustrating. Road construction had brought the cars to a standstill that extended for miles, and I was forced to slowly weave between overheating vehicles and angry drivers to reach the heart of the city where I finally found a hotel for the night.

A hint to fellow travelers: When staying at the Doubletree Inn adjacent to the Florida Capital Building, you may be asked whether you want an interior or street-view room. The correct answer is always: "street view." Finding myself in desperate need of a good night's sleep, I chose the interior, assuming it would be quieter. After checking in, I lugged my bicycle and gear up the elevator to my room, stripped everything off my pale, flabby body except my skintight Lycra biking shorts, and threw back the curtain anticipating a nice view of an interior courtyard or a relaxing sunset.

Instead, I discovered that what I had expected to be a window was something far more surreal: a floor-to-ceiling glass wall with unobstructed views of an interior-parking garage. On the other side, less than five feet away, was a very surprised family (husband, wife and two young children) standing next to their parked car with suitcases and bags in hand.

We stared at each other in paralyzed silence as my brain tried to process what I was seeing. As I looked from person to person, I imagined the children asking: "Daddy, why is that man dressed like that?" Then, as I grabbed for a towel to cover myself, the family averted their eyes, hurriedly climbed into the car, and drove off.

I don't know who was more embarrassed, but I'm fairly certain those children will require many years of psychotherapy as a result of this incident.

The following morning, the rain started again. The hotel desk clerk helped me with directions to a bicycle shop across town where I hoped to find some rain covers for my panniers, which I had discovered weren't entirely waterproof. By the time I arrived at the shop, I was saturated and, of course, the store was closed for the day. Neither of us had thought to call to check on its business hours. With no other choice, I headed out into the rain and, for the next several hours, fought chaotic traffic, narrow cracked streets, stoplights, and distracted pedestrians under oversized umbrellas as I tried to get out of the city and into a safer, more relaxed setting. It felt like an endless journey, as if I were trying to escape the pull of some type of urban black hole.

Hours later, under a light rain, I reached the small town of Quincy and walked my bicycle around the town square looking for a place to eat and rest my legs. A faded Coca-Cola mural covering a large brick building was a reminder of the town's unique history. When the Coca-Cola Company went public in 1919, at least two-dozen Quincy citizens were shareholders because of their relationship with one of the company's earliest financiers. As a result, they became instant millionaires, helping to raise the economic fortunes of Quincy and the surrounding area.

Sadly, this prosperity was in the distant past. The town around me was run down and decaying with only a few architectural reminders of its glory days. A number of the shops near the square were vacant or had few customers and outdated merchandise. The economic collapse of 2008 had very clearly taken its toll on Quincy, and I wondered if the community would ultimately face the same fate as the Weeden Island people.

Across the street from the Gadsen County courthouse, I found a small café called "Miss Helen's." I stood outside, chilled and soaking, reading the menu and trying to decide whether to enter, when a handsome woman walked up next to me: "Why don't y'all come on in and get warm and out of this rain?"

I looked around, still a bit unsure, when she offered her hand and said, "People around here call me 'Miss Helen.' My husband and I own this place."

"Come on, come on," she prodded in a gentle voice. "You can bring your bike in as well."

I couldn't resist her charm and followed her inside, leaned my bicycle against a wall, and sat down at a small table. For the next hour, I relaxed in this paragon of Southern hospitality. Miss Helen and her husband made me feel immediately at ease, almost at home, with their polite conversation and attentive service.

They also poured a mighty tasty sweet tea, and I could tell from the first glass that I would become intimate friends with this traditional Southern libation. In fact, I even gave serious thought to attaching an IV drip containing this magical elixir to my handlebars to fend off dehydration as I rode.

It was early afternoon when I finished my lunch, thanked Miss Helen, and stood up to leave. As I did, her husband approached me.

"Do you think you could come take a look at my bicycle?" he asked. "I want to see what you think of it."

It was a strange request. Because he was a bit portly and looked to be in his late seventies, he didn't strike me as a cyclist, but I followed him down a dark hallway and into a large storeroom where he showed me an expensive mountain bike that had been retrofitted for touring.

"What do you think I can get for it?

"That's a nice bike. I've seen ones like it sell for around $1,500 in good condition where I live. How often do you ride it?" I asked.

Putting his hands on his ample stomach, he laughed and said: "Do I look like I ride, son? I haven't been on a bicycle in decades. Nah, nah, another guy riding cross-country like you came through 'bout a year ago. While he was eatin', he got a call and found out that he had a family emergency back home in St. Louis. He left his bicycle here, and Miss Helen and I closed the restaurant and drove him to the airport in Tallahassee."

"What happened to him?" I asked.

"Don't know. Never heard from the guy again," he said in quiet voice as he stared at the bicycle. "Figured he would call and tell us where to ship it, but it's been over a year now."

Later, as I pedaled away from Quincy, this conversation kept coming to mind, and I found myself thinking about that bicycle gathering dust in the darkened storeroom. It left me with an unsettled feeling about the many ways my ride could come to an early end.

My planned destination for the night was DeFuniak Springs. Despite the continued poor weather, as I headed toward the town the scenery was enchanting. In breaks of light between the somber clouds and mist, I'd catch quick glimpses of intense beauty. It was like an old Kodak carousel slide show—a captivating view of lush saw grass along a deep green bayou and then gray darkness, a piercing ray of sunlight illuminating a century-old abandoned home, and then darkness again.

As I rode a rusted trestle bridge over a muddy creek, I looked down to see a blue heron and a great white egret. Startled by my arrival, they flapped their large wings and flew off in a double helix only a few feet above my head. Along many portions of the route, dark swamps surrounded by stately oaks lined the roadway. They looked ethereal with their gray moss waving in the wind and the leaves on the black pools spinning in mosaics of slowly changing patterns as if through a child's toy kaleidoscope.

Pedaling toward DeFuniak, I wove through a series of small nondescript towns with names like "Chipley," "Bonifay," and "Ponce de Leon." The names, however, appeared far more interesting than the communities themselves, which usually consisted of a dozen or so wooden or brick one-story homes with flags over the porches, a few churches, a gas station, a memorial to local veterans, and, perhaps, a mini-mart or local fast food restaurant. They were scenes reminiscent of John Mellencamp's song "*Pink Houses*" and almost without conscious thought I found myself mouthing the lyrics: "Ain't that America home of the free, little pink houses for you and me."

One of the more memorable towns I rode through was Caryville, Florida. A large hand-painted sign celebrated its fame as the "Worm Fiddlin' Capital of the World." Also known as "snoring" or "doodling," worm fiddling is a method by which fishermen in some parts of the South collect their bait. In Caryville this was accomplished by driving a short stake into the ground and then slowly rubbing the top of it with a piece of iron, brick, or roughened wood. The vibrations drove worms to the surface where they were collected by hand and sold by the pound to local bait shops. As I pedaled past, I thought to myself that there may be stranger ways to make a living, but I wasn't sure what they were.

Most of my route in this section of the Florida Panhandle was identified as the "Lawton Chiles, Jr. Trail." Before he became governor, Chiles was a member of the Florida House of Representatives and decided to run for the United States Senate in 1970. To generate name recognition and media coverage, Chiles walked more than 1,000 miles from Pensacola to Key West. Along the way, he met with constituents, gave impromptu stump speeches, and walked through the soles of several pairs of boots. This unique method of campaigning earned him the nickname "Walkin' Lawton." And he won the election.

While it would be nice to witness that type of commitment from today's politicians, I found it difficult to imagine. With the Internet and social networking sites, politicians today have an easier time promoting themselves than Governor Chiles did—at least it would appear so from the barrage of emails I receive from candidates prior to each election. As an additional benefit, they also get to save on their shoe budgets.

With all respect to Governor Chiles, a more apt name for the route I was travelling might have been the "Road Kill Highway." Animal carcasses littered the roadway, as if I had arrived immediately after a horrific interspecies battle. Often I would smell carrion long before it was visible. As a macabre distraction, I decided to keep track of each animal corpse I passed. I counted mangled bodies of dogs of every size and breed, as well as cats, birds, foxes, raccoons, and possums. They continued for mile after mile. After my tally reached the triple digits, I had to quit counting, as I was starting to make myself nauseated.

Strangely, I would see road kill littering the roadway almost continuously in the following weeks as I travelled through Florida, Mississippi, Alabama, and Louisiana until I reached the Texas border where the carnage came to an end. The change was oddly noticeable. People I met offered a number of interesting theories about it. They ranged from "Got a lotta drunk drivers here in the South" to "Louisiana politicians are all corrupt. They take all the money, and there's nothing left for road cleanup." My favorite: "Texans will cook and eat anything."

Rather than dining on road kill, near the town of Argyle I found a small, run-down market and pulled over to buy something more nutritious. Before starting the ride, I had assumed that I would have abundant access to healthy food, especially while travelling through the farming and fishing communities of the South. I envisioned frequently stopping at roadside vegetable stands for replenishment as I pedaled. The reality was that there were no vegetable stands and few true grocery stores along my route, the kind you see with overflowing bunkers of fresh fruit and vegetables. Instead, I found gas station mini-marts or large Walmart-type stores (usually on the outskirts of a community), but rarely anything else except an occasional market like this one, which was clearly on its last legs.

As I entered the store, I noticed I was the only patron. The only other person was the clerk, a young woman on her cell phone engaged in a nasty argument with her boyfriend or, possibly, husband. She was so distracted I don't think she even registered my presence.

As I walked along the aisles, I discovered that not only were there no vegetables or fruits, but that everything was boxed, wrapped, or processed. A check of the refrigerated section revealed a small selection of dairy products and lunchmeats. But they all looked risky. Is baloney supposed to have purple streaks? Most of the items I considered were covered in a layer of dust, and many were well past their "sell by" date.

I was witnessing economic market dynamics in action, and it was painful to see. As large discount mass merchandisers move into a community, they put tremendous financial pressure on smaller competitors. Stores like this one can't compete on price or selection, or turn inventory as quickly. As a result, to stay afloat, they sell more pre-packaged goods and cut corners by holding products past their expiration date. In many cases, even this isn't enough to survive, and the businesses fail. It was one of those sad realities of small-town America that I would see repeated in towns across the country.

I combed through the store in search of nutrition, and when I couldn't find something healthy, I succumbed to my caloric cravings. With a small measure of guilt, I purchased a bag of Cheetos that was eight months past its expiration date and a can of iced tea that required me to blow the dust off the lid before cracking it open. The clerk rang me up without a pause in her telephonic diatribe, and I walked out taking one last look at the dingy, empty store. Then I saddled my bike and rode off feeling strangely despondent.

Toward the end of this long day of riding, my legs, arms, and back ached, and I was feeling emotionally drained and discouraged by the poor weather, road kill, and marginal food. My mind was numb, and I became easily distracted. For example, as I approached a sign announcing the town of DeFuniak Springs, I started thinking things like: "DeFuniak? Looks kind of like 'The Funk'." The next think I knew, I had the old R&B group Parliament's hit "Give Up the Funk" running through my brain in an endless loop.

There are various names for the phenomenon: "earworms," "humbugs," or, my personal favorite, "tune wedgies." It's when a song comes to mind, usually one that is mundane and monotonous, and your brain locks on it like a terrier with a tennis ball. I even tried listening to a Bill Moyer podcast on banking reform to cleanse my mental palette, but nothing worked. I couldn't get the song out of my head, and the repetition was challenging my sanity.

In an effort to lift my spirits, I made the decision that the following day would be a beach day. I would detour off my planned route and head south to the coast, along the Gulf of Mexico and then into Pensacola. That would make for a more pleasing ride. Unless, of course, I thought of another song from the 1970s—perhaps something by The Starland Vocal Band: "Gonna find my baby, gonna hold her tight, gonna grab some afternoon delight…."

Oh, crap.

four

DeFuniak Springs, Florida, to Gulfport, Mississippi
Total Ride Mileage: 572

The detour to the Gulf Coast was a good decision. After leaving DeFuniak Springs the next morning, the ride was flat and for much of it I even had the luxury of a bicycle lane, a rarity in this part of the country. The weather remained unsettled; sunshine vied with cold blustery winds that bit into my cheeks. It felt odd to be riding along postcard beautiful beaches under a clear sky while wearing multiple layers of clothing to stay warm. Much of the ride I spent crouched in the handlebar drops trying to minimize wind resistance. As I rode, flashes of gold appeared on the periphery of my view—flocks of yellow-rumped warblers scattering like leaves before my wheels.

Passing through Destin, Florida, I continued across Okaloosa Island with the Gulf on my left. For days, I had been riding through small towns on two-lane country roads. Now, I was back in the world of fast food restaurants, strip malls, and 20-story condominiums. It was jarring—as if I had gone from 1970 to the present in the space of 40 miles.

I kept pedaling until I reached Fort Walton Beach, a Gulf Coast resort town where I checked into a dated family-oriented hotel while trying to understand the clerk over sunburned, sand-covered children in bathing suits, rampaging through the lobby followed by frazzled, screaming parents. The place was a perfectly preserved piece of mid-20th century Americana. My room was decorated with musty drapes, faux colonial pressboard furniture, and drab floral wallpaper, reminding me of a place where Lucille and Ricky Ricardo would have vacationed in the 1950s. There was even a dilapidated shuffleboard court outside my room.

The following day began with a 6 a.m. wake-up courtesy of the family next door, who, by the sound of it, must have been practicing the fine art of Greco-Roman wrestling. To make matters worse, I stumbled into the bathroom, grabbed what I thought was a tube of toothpaste, and applied a copious amount of Desitin diaper rash cream to my toothbrush and began brushing until my cerebral cortex awoke and signaled that something wasn't quite right.

For the uninitiated, most serious bicyclists use a lubricant affectionately known as "Butt Butter" to decrease friction in one's riding shorts. Unfortunately, I had used all of mine in the first week of riding because of the crappy weather (wet shorts = extra chafing) and had yet to find a bicycle shop with any in stock. Riding without "Butt Butter" had done its damage. In fact, if you had seen me naked from behind, you would have mistaken me for *papio ursinus* (i.e. a red-assed baboon).

To alleviate my condition, I turned to that childhood friend, Desitin; despite what it may lack as toothpaste, it is a suitable and soothing replacement. The big drawback to it, however, was that the oily white paste bled through my black cycling shorts. On one occasion, after I got up from a counter seat at a Waffle House restaurant, I heard a snicker. When I turned, I saw a heavyset man in overalls in a booth enjoying a laugh with a friend and pointing to my shorts. Looking down, I noticed the large white patch on my backside.

On the other hand, the unique Desitin aroma must have triggered some sort of latent maternal instinct in the women I encountered. I'm convinced waitresses become far more attentive. Everywhere I ate, I heard: "Honey, you need an extra slice of pie!" or "Why don't you rest a spell and I'll get you another big glass of sweet tea." It made me wonder whether there might be a market opportunity for a Desitin-scented cologne for middle-aged men.

By noon, I was riding over Three-Mile Bridge and into the city of Pensacola. I had lived there briefly as a young child when my father was stationed at the Naval Air Station attending flight school. As I pedaled, family memories filled me—my crew-cut father in his bathing trunks running through the surf with me in his arms, my mother standing behind the stove making pancakes, my brother asleep in his playpen—but these came only from brittle, scalloped-edged photographs in a childhood scrapbook. Nothing looked familiar.

I coasted slowly through the small downtown section until I saw a nearby public park with large banners indicating that it was the site of the annual

Florida State barbecue competition. The streets surrounding the park were lined with dozens of high-end mobile homes and trucks towing various types of barbecue apparatuses, from stainless steel computerized models to grills created with little more than a welding torch and an empty oil barrel. From their license plates, it was clear that this event attracted participants from around the country. The smell of hickory smoke, sizzling beef, pork, chicken, alligator, and hot dripping fat filled the air. Stopping my bike there was an easy decision.

For me, the food pyramid is composed entirely of meat, with bacon holding its exalted place at the top. Mama Dillon didn't raise her boys to be vegans. So, after days of fast and freeze-dried food, I was in a state of culinary ecstasy.

I walked my bicycle through the growing crowd, listening to contestants discussing sauce ingredients (always mentioning an undisclosed "little sumthin' special") and grilling techniques ("Ya need to turn it with a quick flip of the wrist"). Many competitors, with names like "Lotta Bull Barbecue" and "Skin & Bones Barbecue," proudly displayed trophies, large blue or red ribbons, engraved pewter dishes, and signs that exclaimed things like: "3-Time American Royal Grand Champion!" It was the perfect excuse for lunch, and I loaded up a large plate of assorted barbecued meats, red beans, and biscuits and topped it off with a large glass of cold sweet tea. Then, with a full stomach, I stretched out on the lawn for a snooze in the warm sun.

As I drifted off, I thought about how I would soon pass a forest near Foley, Alabama, where my father was forced to bail out of his plane and parachute to the ground during a naval training exercise. The thought made me reflect on the span of his military career and how difficult it must have been for him and others in the military to frequently be away from their spouses and children.

After only a few weeks on the road, I missed my family intensely and thought of them frequently as I pedaled. We would exchange daily calls, email or text messages, but it wasn't enough to alleviate my longing. Yet for more than a decade, my father was called away from his family for six to nine months each year on dangerous military deployments. During those periods, the only way he could communicate with us was by way of infrequently delivered letters or an occasional scratchy, brief "ship to shore" shortwave radio relay call.

I really don't know how he did it.

Given my melancholy mood, it lifted my spirits to receive a message from my father-in-law indicating that some friends of his, Jim and Kay, were vacationing on my route in a beautiful apartment overlooking the Gulf of Mexico, and they had invited me to stay the night. Although I didn't know them well, the chance to spend an evening in a place other than a lonely motel room or rundown campground was irresistible.

After leaving the park and pedaling for a couple of hours, I finally reached Jim and Kay's apartment. When I knocked on the door, they welcomed me as if I was family, and after I soaked in a long hot shower, we enjoyed a wonderful meal and a bottle of wine and spent the evening together discussing family, friends, politics, movies and books. It was deeply nourishing to enjoy more than the superficial conversations I had experienced with waitresses, motel desk clerks, and other cyclists over the previous days. We talked for hours, until finally I could keep my head vertical no longer and headed off to sleep in a "real" bed.

When I awoke the next morning, I had to resist my friends' enticements to stay for a few more days. They prepared a delicious breakfast to win me over; however, I knew that if I remained longer, I would be tempted to declare my trip at an end, kick back on the beach for a few days, and then book a flight home. Thus, it was with much reluctance that I finally left them in the late morning and rode toward Fort Morgan, Alabama, to catch the ferry across Mobile Bay.

As I pedaled, a stream of loaded vehicles passed by with license plates from Minnesota, New Jersey, Missouri, and Illinois on their way to the ferry, snowbirds heading north. They left behind empty pastel-colored rental homes with names like "Our Time," "Sea Shadow," and "Neptune's Crew," all awaiting the arrival of students on spring break the following week. This was the quiet "elbow" season between the retirees returning home from their winter vacations and the onslaught of college students seeking sand, sunshine, and libations.

I decided to take it easy that day and ride at a slower pace. As I pedaled, I grew aware that I was feeling something more than normal fatigue. My body was still voicing its objection to the constant physical exertion, but after a few hours on the road, I realized that I had also developed a nasty chest cold. I felt old, beaten, and achy and the ferry to Dauphin Island was a welcome respite. It would be the only portion of my journey, other than crossing the Mississippi River, where I would not be moving using my own power.

As we motored slowly across the placid waters of the bay, we passed dozens of natural gas drilling platforms. Alabama ranks in the top 10 of states for natural gas production, and much of it flows from these wells. They sat in only about 10 to 15 feet of water but had gas pipes that descended more than 20,000 feet. Citizens of Alabama had become accustomed to these platforms, which were first installed in the late 1970s, and none of the ferry crew I spoke with expressed any concern about negative impacts to the environment. In fact, one of them said that local fisherman appreciated the wells because they provided a plentiful habitat for fish; as evidence, he pointed to a number of small fishing boats anchored near the long legs of one of the platforms.

As he spoke, I looked off the stern and watched as a group of dolphins reveled in the ferry's wake. Dolphins and gas platforms—it all felt rather incongruous.

Upon docking at Dauphin Island, I pedaled to Fort Gaines. Along with Fort Monroe, on the eastern side of the bay, Fort Gaines was a strategically important position for the Confederate Army in protecting the city of Mobile during the Civil War. It was near here, in 1864, that Admiral David Farragut of the Union Navy issued the famous words "Damn the torpedoes. Full speed ahead" as his naval forces (along with a separate army contingent) broke through Confederate defenses. Fort Gaines also served as the base for the British campaign against the city of Mobile during the War of 1812.

I thought back to when I studied this military post in my high school history class. I imagined it as a grand, impressive historical site. To see it in person, small and still, was a testament to the true value of travel—to bring to reality what you have seen only in your imagination or read about in a book.

A bit past dusk, I at last struggled into Bayou La Batre (pop. 2,300), the self-proclaimed "Seafood Capital of Alabama." After checking into a motel and a quick shower, I asked the motel clerk to recommend a place for dinner. He directed me to the Lighthouse Restaurant, claiming that it was the only decent eatery in town. To get there required another five miles of riding on unknown roads with the sun rapidly setting. This was an example of the downside of life on a bicycle. When I arrived at the end of a tiring day of pedaling, it was always a challenge to shower, dress, and get back on the saddle again—even if for only a few miles. How I longed to be able to hop into a car on those nights.

When I entered the restaurant, it was crowded with local fishermen and oyster farmers taking their families out for weekend dining. This was without doubt the happening place in town. After a brief wait, a waitress walked me through the restaurant to a booth and took my order, and within a few minutes, I was served a feast of pan-fried grouper, coleslaw, hush puppies, and…wait for it… sweet tea!

Football in the South, especially high school and college football, is not just a sports pastime—it borders on a religion. Nowhere was this more apparent than in Alabama where it seemed almost every home or car was decorated with a flag or bumper sticker supporting the University of Alabama's Crimson Tide football team. This restaurant was no different, displaying numerous team banners and pennants. As I enjoyed my grouper, I gazed at the wall opposite me. Located in the middle of it, like a religious icon, was a life-size bust of Coach Bear Bryant, the former coach of the Crimson Tide. To give you a sense of the intensity of the football faithful in this area, Coach Bryant had been deceased for more than 25 years.

It was difficult navigating back to the motel after I finished dinner. The sun had fully set and the absence of ambient light and the tall trees along the road created the impression of riding through a black, sinister tunnel. My flashlight was ineffective at throwing a beam more than a few feet in the intense darkness, so, I turned it off and rode with only my thoughts for distraction. What were my children doing? I wondered. Was Liz overloaded with home responsibilities? How was the rest of my family? Were they thinking of me or preoccupied with their own lives? My cold was worsening and it was clearly affecting my spirits. I felt battered and ill and longed for the ministrations of my loving wife. When I at last reached the motel, I made the decision to forego riding and to spend most of the next day sleeping.

It was late in the afternoon when I fully awoke. Feeling marginally better, I dressed and decided to go for a walk and a bit of exploring. In front of my hotel, I stopped a woman and asked for directions to the downtown district or any other places of interest.

Her response? "Honey, there ain't nothin' to see in this town."

As I walked around, I had to agree with her. Bayou La Batre was a small town that had seen better days. Once a thriving commercial center for ship-building, fishing, and oyster farming, it had even served as a location for the movie *Forrest Gump*. Then Hurricane Katrina ravaged the area.

Like most Americans, I watched my television with a profound sense of anguish as Hurricane Katrina decimated New Orleans and the surrounding region. Yet a small part of me rationalized that, as with every disaster reported in the media, it couldn't have been as bad as it was portrayed. I had lived a few miles from the epicenter of the 1989 Loma Prieta earthquake in California and recalled how the television reporting magnified the perceptions of damage from that disaster.

But as I walked through Bayou La Batre that day and rode through Mississippi and Louisiana over the following weeks, I would begin to get a glimpse of the reach and enormity of Katrina's destructive force. It was of a scale that no television coverage could ever adequately convey.

Five years after Katrina, Bayou La Batre still hadn't recovered. Its citizens were out of work and hurting; their median annual income was less than $25,000 per household. Along the streets I saw vacant lots, boarded businesses, piles of oysters shells from an abandoned shucking plant, and rusted equipment alongside an ancient (and now abandoned) shrimp processing operation. It was a community close to disappearing.

My wanderings did nothing to lift my spirit, but they did give me an appetite. I didn't have the energy to ride my bicycle again to the Lighthouse Restaurant, but there was a place to eat within walking distance of my motel. Unfortunately, it was a video rental store that also offered "fresh heated pizza"—not "oven baked" or "home made," but "fresh heated." When not even pizza can excite, you know you've hit bottom. It amounted to a rather depressing day and served to amplify my already discouraged spirits.

The following morning, I still didn't feel well, but I had to get out of Bayou La Batre. No offense to the citizens of the town, but I was in need of a change in scenery and didn't think my stomach could handle another night of pizza prepared by a video rental store clerk. So after breakfast, I departed Bayou La Batre and rode for several hours before crossing into Mississippi and reaching the city of Biloxi.

The Biloxi beach was one long strip of sand the whitest color imaginable, almost painful to the eyes. But as I pedaled, I had the distant sense that something was missing; that something was not quite right. It was almost too perfect—just miles of pristine zinc white sand against a denim blue sea, all of it empty.

As I looked more closely, I realized that there were none of the trashy bars, aged hotels, or garish tourist shops that I had seen along the sand in most other beach towns in the United States. Pedaling farther, I noticed opposite the beach stately old homes surrounded by portable scaffolding, large brick buildings propped with wood bracing, and businesses in the process of being demolished.

Then I realized that this was all the result of Hurricane Katrina. It had erased everything that had once existed along the beach.

Late in the day, I stopped at a bicycle store in Gulfport to have my front wheel aligned. As the mechanic wrenched on my spokes, I asked him about Katrina.

"Were you here during the storm?"

"Yep. It was like nothing you could imagine," he said with his voice trailing off. "But I was lucky and able to get to safety with my family. Thankfully, our place didn't have much damage."

"What about the shop?" I asked.

"Oh yeah. This is all new. Come with me for a second," he said putting down his wrench and gesturing me to follow him out to the street.

As we stood outside the shop, he pointed up the road to a large brick building. "See the wall of that building?" he asked. "The highpoint of storm surge was 28 feet right there." Then with a pause he said: "And that building is almost two miles inland from the Gulf."

I could find nothing to say in response. Any words would have been trite and trivial. It was clear that I would never truly understand what the people of this area had been through, although I would continue to get a sense of it in the days ahead.

Section 2

Facing Constant Chafing and Inclement Weather,
Our Hero Experiences the Dog Days of the Deep South.

(Mississippi and Louisiana)

five

Gulfport, Mississippi, to Fontainebleau State Park, Louisiana
Total Ride Mileage: 643

That night I checked into a small chain motel, still feeling unwell and increasingly concerned that I had developed pneumonia. Everything ached. Everything. And when I coughed, I sounded like a leopard seal with a four-pack-a-day cigarette habit. I called my doctor and, after listening to my symptoms, she prescribed antibiotics and grounded me for the day. Normally, I would have argued with her, but I felt like shit. There's just no other word for it. I slept a solid 14 hours, which suggested she was a good diagnostician.

When I awoke the next morning, I weighed the physical benefit of remaining in bed against the mental anguish of continuing to watch the vapid abyss of early morning American television. After several hours of advertisements for hemorrhoid cream, medical alert bracelets ("I've fallen and I can't get up"), celebrity makeovers, and Latin soap operas, I couldn't take it any longer. The decision was easy—get riding. As additional inducement, I decided to first stop at the Krispy Kreme Doughnuts store located across the street.

A fixture of the South, Krispy Kreme was founded in the 1930s by a Kentucky businessman who acquired a secret recipe for the yeast-filled doughnuts that he delivered by bicycle. Given the symmetry of this historical nugget—bicycles and doughnuts—I found it completely appropriate to order two gut busters along with a large cup of coffee. My waitress, after sizing me up, threw in a third for free: "Honey, you look like y'all be needin' another one." She was right. It was exactly what I needed. Within 10 minutes, I was trembling uncontrollably from the combination of cold weather, sugar, and caffeine and decided it was time to get back on the bike.

I travelled for a couple of hours on two-lane roads before chafing got the best of me. Because my riding pants were constantly wet from sweat and the damp weather, my upper legs were raw and beginning to bleed slightly, creating an "inner thigh tartare" from the constant rubbing against my seat. In search of relief, I decided to stop at a store to see if I could find some type of cream or lubricant.

Having worked for a large corporation with employees and customers around the world, I've always understood the need to be sensitive to local cultures and traditions. But given that I was traveling in my home country and not abroad, I hadn't considered this on my ride until I stopped that morning at a small market at the intersection of two remote Mississippi farm roads.

When you begin cycling as a recreational rider, it's normal to shy away from traditional cycling clothing like black Lycra riding shorts and tight-fitting jerseys. They feel silly at first, but as you transition to more serious riding, you begin to understand that there are good reasons for this type of clothing, or "kit," as it is called: to minimize chafing, to reduce wind resistance and to increase comfort. However, when riding through small rural towns that don't have a culture of cycling, I found that I needed to be aware of how strange (and possibly offensive) my attire appeared.

Entering this little grocery store, I walked to the counter in my full biking regalia— helmet, multicolored jersey, tight black shorts, fingerless gloves, funky patterned cycling socks—and in my deepest, most masculine voice asked: "Excuse me, do you have any Desitin diaper rash cream?" The young female clerk took a long look in my direction, but said nothing. Absolutely nothing. She just stared.

After a few awkward moments, I looked uneasily over my shoulder to see four very large men in overalls and work boots—think, size 18 necks, minimum—giving me the "You're not from around here boy, are ya?" stare. Then it dawned on me that to these hardworking farmers and ranchers, the idea of recreational cycling was as alien as a gym membership, and my clothes only made matters worse.

The clerk at last pointed down an aisle, and I sheepishly retrieved a small tube of Desitin. As I made my purchase, I briefly considered asking for a tin of Skoal chewing tobacco, a couple of boxes of 12 gauge shotgun shells, a bottle of Jack, and directions to the nearest tattoo parlor. Instead, I made my purchase, quietly exited the store, and decided that from then on, I would carry long pants and a loose shirt in my front panniers to throw over my bike kit whenever I stopped.

My travels that morning took me through veils of thick fog that dampened the noise of the occasional car and made the surroundings look ghostly. Reminders of Katrina were everywhere—restored century-old mansions adjacent to the broken remains of house foundations; brick staircases that led to nowhere; and once crowded asphalt city parking lots, now given up to weeds.

Katrina was not just a memory in this part of the country.

Perhaps it was witnessing the extent of the damage from Katrina, or maybe it was my nagging cold, but by the time I crossed the bridge into the town of Bay St. Louis, I was feeling rather downhearted. My spirits lifted a bit when in front of a local laundromat I connected with Don, the rider I had met a week earlier in Florida, who was doing his laundry and wolfing down a McDonald's Egg McMuffin sandwich. We had been keeping track of each other over the previous days through messages and had agreed to meet at this laundromat, which was identified on our maps.

I felt a growing camaraderie with Don as I listened to him ramble through his experiences since we had last seen each other. In Biloxi, Don had pulled his bicycle and trailer under the roof of a building to wait out a downpour. A battered old pickup pulled alongside him in the rain, and its driver, an elderly and destitute looking man, rolled down a foggy window and stuck his hand out with a few crumpled dollar bills. He said, "Son, you look like you need some help." Don, surprised at the offer, protested that he wasn't homeless and in fact had money, but the man pushed it on him anyway and drove off. Later that evening, Don put the money to good use when he bought a round of beer with it for his fellow bar patrons and had them join him in a toast to his unknown benefactor.

After we finished swapping stories, Don and I sat on a nearby bench and, as he munched on his McMuffin, we pored over our maps, comparing our planned routes for the next few days. I was going to try to make it to Madisonville for the evening, but Don suggested we meet near Lake Pontchartrain and camp together at Fontainebleau State Park.

As I got up to leave, I couldn't resist pointing at his McMuffin. "Do you really eat those things?"

"Man, it's the weirdest thing. I never used to eat crap like this, but a couple of weeks ago, I grabbed one for breakfast, and I felt really good all day. I don't know if it's the fat or the calories, but there is something in these that really makes me feel stronger. Since then, I try to start each day with at least two in my belly before I get pedaling. Want to try a bite?" he said as he offered it to me.

Don clearly had developed an almost reverential feeling toward this mainstay of fast food cuisine. But he wasn't alone in his obsession. Many of the other riders I would meet expressed similar cravings or believed that certain foods had talismanic qualities and would ensure a safer or easier day of riding. For some it was oatmeal; for others, doughnuts or Slim Jim beef jerky sticks. I had my own as well. Strangely, it turned out to be chocolate milk, something I hadn't had in years. Also, cold beer. Damn, I did love a cold one at the end of long day of pedaling.

I politely declined Don's offer, left him to finish his laundry, and headed down the highway. For the next four hours, I traveled a remote roadway dodging rain showers as I wound through dense, desolate bayous before entering what had, due to the recent Super Bowl success of the New Orleans Saints football team, become known as the "Who Dat Nation"—the state of Louisiana.

I once heard a resident of this area interviewed about the impact of Hurricane Katrina. As she said, "The English language does not yet have a word that adequately conveys the destruction." Travelling through the area five years after the storm, I began to get an idea of what she meant. Katrina remained a presence along every road I traveled—entire forests with tree tops snapped off like match heads, enormous mounds of vehicles and debris piled on secluded dirt roads, a rotting fishing boat lying on its side in the middle of a group of pine trees more than a mile from the nearest waterway.

Still, the bayous possessed a special beauty. Large blue herons floated in the air like kites above a child, and the high grass waved slowly in the breeze as if nature was beckoning me forward. In one place, I spotted a large tree lying across an obsidian-tinted swamp. It had an unusual-looking bark: glistening olive black with a scalloped surface. As I stopped to take a photograph, the bark quickly dissolved into the water, causing me to question for a moment what I was seeing. Then I realized that it was more than a dozen small turtles sunning themselves before being startled by my arrival.

The beauty and solitude of this place made me long for my family, but it wasn't for loneliness—the daily contact with my wife and children and the constant flow of messages from friends kept me connected. Instead, it was the realization that I would never be able to properly convey what I was seeing, experiencing, and feeling.

Some things remain all your own.

In the late afternoon, I located a scenic pathway called the "Tammany Trace," a bike trail built upon the remnants of an unused rail bed of the Illinois Central Railroad. For 30 miles I followed it as it wound through pine forests and quiet suburban neighborhoods before passing near a small local market where I decided to stop and buy some food for the evening.

Grabbing a basket, I tapped down the aisles in my bicycle cleats trying not to slip on the ancient but well-polished linoleum floors. As I did, an elderly woman, perhaps in her early 80s, approached me. She was dressed very formally with a long dark felt coat covering a floral-patterned dress. Her gray hair was neatly styled in a bun under a black velvet and lace hat. "Young man, are you doing a bicycle ride?" she asked in a wavering voice.

"Yes, ma'am," I replied.

"Where are you riding from?"

"I started in Florida, and I'm riding across the southern United States to my home, which is about 50 miles south of San Francisco."

"Oh, my Lord, that's a long way! Do you have family there?"

"Yes, I have a wife and three teenage children."

"Who are you travelling with? You aren't by yourself are you?"

"Yes, ma'am, I am," I said.

Then, for the next few minutes, I found myself releasing an almost unstoppable river of stories about my travels—the people I had met, the challenging weather, the captivating scenery—as this woman listened with rapt interest, while holding her shopping basket in the crook of her arm. When I finished, she reached out with her gloved hands and took hold of mine. Looking deep into my eyes for a few moments, she said with quiet, tender words, "I hope you have a wonderful journey, and I will pray for your safety."

There are moments in our lives that can be replayed in our minds at will, almost as if a camera had filmed the scene. This was one of those instances for me. I was enveloped by this woman's sense of calm and warmth and felt an intense, almost maternal connection. I wanted to spend more time with her. As I looked into her eyes, I imagined sitting on the wooden porch of an older but well-kept home, drinking sweet tea and listening to stories of her life. But something inside me sensed that it would be impolite to say more. So, after a few moments, I released her hands, thanked her, and watched as she walked slowly away down the aisle.

Don caught up with me at a campsite in Fontainebleau State Park late in the evening. While he cooked dinner, I shared with him the day's Road Kill Report, which consisted of a beautiful barn owl, two armadillos (the first I had ever seen in my life), and an extremely large wild boar—large enough that I almost rethought the idea of camping that evening.

Over beer, cheese and crackers, and a freeze-dried stew that "crunched" because it was not thoroughly cooked, we shared stories until close to midnight. His were definitely more interesting than mine. It was as if we were engaged in a verbal version of the child's game roshambo, with his tales always ending up as "paper" to my "rock." I'd talk about my many times backpacking in the Sierras, and he would casually mention that he lived much of the year in a remote cabin in the Alaskan wilderness. I'd recount a number of my kayak trips in California, Mexico, and Canada and he would respond with a tale about one of his adventures as a whitewater guide on the Colorado River. When we spoke about careers, I described with modest pride my work as an attorney for a number of high tech companies. He responded with humorous episodes from his early days as a New York State Trooper or from his current job as a construction manager—in Antarctica, where he once even borrowed a bicycle and rode a couple of laps around the South Pole for fun.

As we talked, storm clouds and lightning slowly drew closer from over the dark horizon, and then the wind began to rise. Acknowledging that we were in for some strong weather, we polished off the last of the beer and decided to call it a night.

Don and I embodied the opposing philosophies of bicycle touring. I was a minimalist, carrying only what I could hold in my panniers, trading weight for speed. Don was prepared for anything with gear stacked high in the trailer he was towing behind his bike.

That night his team won. After we went to bed, a powerful storm hit, releasing several inches of rainfall in a few hours. Don slept undisturbed in his three-person tent, oblivious to the conditions outside, while I was awake almost until daybreak. In the confines of my bivy sack, it was as if I were sleeping in a large trash bag with multiple high-pressure fire hoses spraying me throughout the night. Although I remained dry, I felt the heavy rain pelt my body through the thin nylon of the bivy and sensed the cool temperature outside. I spent the night thrashing to get comfortable. Worse yet, in the midst of this deluge, I kept hearing an annoying sound like air escaping from…a leak in my air mattress.

Damn.

six

Fountainebleau State Park to Simmesport, Louisiana
Total Ride Mileage: 805

Don and I were beginning to form a friendship of the road. It was a growing relationship built on shared experiences amassed over miles of asphalt. That, and a deep mutual affection for beer. When he pulled into camp the previous evening I could hear the chilled bottles clinking in his trailer like an adult version of the Good Humor Ice Cream trucks of my youth.

As we left Fontainebleau State Park and headed our separate ways the next morning, I found myself looking forward to intersecting his path again in the following weeks and comparing stories over a few cold ones. But I was also slowly gaining confidence in my ability to manage the new challenges of each day, and I was interested in the other people I would meet over the miles ahead.

Riding on toward Baton Rouge, I passed through a series of small southern towns, each different, yet somehow the same—variations on a theme. In one drive-in style restaurant, a sign advertised "Cooter Brown's Seafood." It brought to mind a game I used to play with a friend who had spent several decades as a kindergarten teacher. Each year she would ask me to guess the most popular names in her classroom. Usually they were ones like "Michael" or "Emma" or "Ethan" or "Madison." Although "Cooter" never made the list, it would get my vote.

Heading down the highway into the center of Baton Rouge made for miserable riding. Enormous eighteen-wheelers and other commercial trucks sped by, only inches from my panniers. On the rare section where a shoulder was available, it took all of my focus to navigate an obstacle course of broken glass, chunks of 4x4 fence posts, car parts, rusty wire, nails, plastic buckets, and assorted pieces of iron.

After two hours of riding through this urban chaos, I gradually came to the conclusion that I was lost. But, because I possess both X and Y chromosomes, I found it unthinkable to ask for help. Instead, I banished the thought to the nether reaches of my mind (located roughly in the same area as knowledge of dishwasher loading and my wedding anniversary) and continued on for another couple of hours before fatigue forced me admit that I needed to ask someone for directions.

Unfortunately, this wasn't something new. I am, as those who know me will attest, "directionally impaired." In my youth, I took a couple of friends backpacking on a well-marked trail in the Sierras that I had hiked several times before. Somehow, I got us lost in the wilderness for 11 days. Even more embarrassing, I was a Boy Scout at the time and had earned the rank of Eagle. On the other hand, my wife, Liz, being a Midwestern girl, has a pitch perfect sense of direction. You could blindfold her, spin her in a centrifuge, and then ask which direction is north, and she would instantly point it out—adjusting for magnetic declination.

Here I was with not just one, but two maps, a compass on my watch, and a GPS system, and I had been hopelessly lost on a major highway for hours. It was even more discouraging when I realized that I had mistakenly overshot downtown Baton Rouge and what was to have been my eagerly anticipated first glimpse of the Mississippi River.

After accepting defeat and getting directions at a small farmers' market (the first I had seen on the trip), I headed north around the outskirts of Baton Rouge through miles of oil refineries, pumping stations, and tanker truck traffic. Riding for hours, the city's industrial outreach gradually receded, and the surroundings became more pastoral as reflected by the handwritten cardboard sign on a telephone pole that advertised "Fresh Coon Meat."

When I reached Port Hudson State Park, I took a break at the visitor center and toured the museum. This location was the site of one of the longest sieges and most murderous battles of the Civil War, during which a Confederate Army of fewer than 7,000 troops prevented more than 30,000 Union soldiers from wresting control of the Mississippi River. Using cannons mounted high on the nearby bluffs above a severe bend in the river, the Confederate Army blocked Union warships and held their opponents in a stalemate for nearly 50 days, resulting in the deaths of more than 12,000 soldiers.

After leaving the museum, I walked alone with my bicycle over the battleground. It was a beautiful Southern day, warm with a slight breeze. As I stepped across the grassy landscape, I felt a conflict between what I saw around me and what I learned in the museum about the horrific battle that had occurred here. During a few weeks in the late spring of 1863 this was a place of acrid smoke, piercing screams, blood-soaked soil, and death. Now it was a place of serenity and peace. It was as if nature had healed the wounds of man.

Twenty miles later, I rolled into St. Francisville, Louisiana (pop. 1,712). If you opened the dictionary to the word "community," a photograph of St. Francisville is all that would be needed to define it. St. Francisville is a small town centered around a local bar and restaurant called the Magnolia Café. Parking my bike, I stepped into the restaurant and struck up a conversation with one of the owners, Kevin, an energetic middle-aged man dressed in faded Levi's and a well-worn plaid shirt. I asked him if there was a place to stay nearby, and he told me that he had a room available in the 3V Tourist Court, also located on the property.

The 3V consisted of five beautifully restored cabins with red roofs, each connected by a narrow carport. Built in the 1930s by the three "V"inci brothers (hence, the name), the cabins were a bit of historical nostalgia from a time when Americans first fell in love with the automobile. Each small cabin (150 square feet) had a bedroom, bathroom, and study area with period furniture. It was rustic, quiet, and perfect for a night of sleep that I so desperately craved.

After I unpacked and showered, I wandered around town enjoying the balmy evening and the antebellum architecture until the sound of a local cover band drew me back to the Magnolia, where I stopped in for dinner. While I was listening to the music and enjoying my meal, Kevin walked over holding a couple of bottles of beer and sat down at my table. He asked me about my ride, and after I answered his questions I inquired about his background and what life was like in this small southern town. Over the course of a wide-ranging conversation, fueled by a few additional beers, he described his early career on the road as a musician and music producer and the rock and country stars he had worked with. Finally, after years of travel and the frustration of trying to make a livelihood in the music business, Kevin decided to take a chance and settle down in St. Francisville and help run the Magnolia. That was more than 25 years ago.

As we talked, enjoyed our drinks, and listened to the music, I looked around at a crowded dining area that radiated warmth, fellowship, and happiness. A group of young girls in Sunday dresses held hands in a circle, giggling and dancing under the pale blue Christmas tree lights that lined the ceiling, while their parents encouraged them from surrounding tables. Nearby, an elderly couple did a lively two-step around the wooden floor as if they were still courting and in their twenties. In the corner, a young pair with tattooed arms draped over each other swayed slowly to a rhythm that only they could hear. Looking around the room, I saw families, farmers, ranchers, and business people of all ages eating, laughing, and enjoying the music. It was as if a small glimpse of the romance of America had been revealed to that boy in the back of the station wagon so many years ago.

I turned to Kevin and said: "You've got something very special here." He just smiled and nodded.

It was late the next morning when I finally departed St. Francisville. It was difficult to leave such an inviting place and I found inconsequential activities to delay my departure—oiling the chain, mending a pannier, rewrapping my handlebar tape—but I had miles to travel and, on that day, something special ahead of me. With great reluctance, I returned my room key, said a warm goodbye to Kevin, and pedaled away, knowing that I would forever hold a bit of the Magnolia Café within me.

After riding only a short few miles on the winding road, I turned a bend and there it was: the Mississippi River. In my youth, I had driven across it several times while traveling the country with family or friends, but I never had the chance to give it more than a 60-mph glance out of the corner of my eye. Now its muddy waters lay a few feet away. Leaning my bicycle against a wooden post, I waited for the ferry to arrive and watched the upstream barge traffic struggle against the broad-shouldered power of the river as it slowly flowed past.

This river was the source of so much American history, culture, and commerce. The water before me carried Andrew Jackson and Abraham Lincoln, as well as thousands of troops during the Civil War. It was the source of inspiration for authors such as Twain, Faulkner, and Tennessee Williams. It provided a critical transportation system on which the country's economic muscle was built. And it delivered that uniquely American form of music, the Delta Blues, to the world. As I took it all in, I felt a surging desire for exploration. (Special note to Liz — please do not read the following sentence.) The Mississippi flows 2,320 miles from its headwaters at Lake Itasca, Minnesota to the Gulf of Mexico; perhaps, I thought, paddling it in a kayak could be my next adventure?

After disembarking the ferry on the west side of the river, I rode in the direction of Simmesport against a vigorous headwind. Stopping at a Walmart in the town of New Roads, I bought a patch kit for my air mattress and then found a gas station to ask for directions. The woman behind the counter was preoccupied with customers and nodded her head in the direction of a local, who had stopped in to pick up a case of beer.

He was short, broad-shouldered, grizzled, and gray, with an impossibly thick Cajun accent. I showed him on my map where I wanted to go, and, in an animated voice, he stuttered rapid-fire directions at me with spittle flying out of his mouth while repeatedly jabbing a sausage-sized finger at the map. Unfortunately, the only thing I could understand was: "Yus wouldn't want tah do dat," a phrase he repeated every few sentences followed by hysterical laughter. After repeatedly asking for clarification, I gave up, nodded my head as if I understood, and thanked him for his help. Walking outside, I used the sleeve of my windbreaker to wipe his saliva from the map and found a patch of grass where I could sit down while I tried to decipher what the "dat" was that he was warning me about. Eventually, I gave up, chose a northwesterly direction, and just started riding again.

For most of the afternoon, the fierce wind of the previous days continued. After traveling for a few hours, I found my bearings and revisited the map, identifying a shorter route in the direction of the Atchafalaya River that would shave 20 miles from the day's ride. Twenty miles might not seem like much from the perspective of someone travelling in a car; however, on a loaded touring bike, it equates to nearly two hours of pedaling—significant after you've already put in five or six that day.

As I headed down a narrow two-lane road in the direction of the river, a man driving the opposite way in a faded old Chevy truck slowed and waved me to a stop. He asked where I was headed, and then warned that the road ahead was dirt and used only by local farmers. More importantly, the ferry that crossed the river was out of operation. If it weren't for the thoughtfulness of this gentleman, my 20-mile shortcut would have ended up adding an additional 40 miles to the day.

Encounters like this were commonplace in the South. It seemed that everyone was friendly and looked out for one another—even a Lycra-encased stranger. This differed from my experience in the urban centers of the country where I had lived for most of my life; there, suspicion is the default emotion when interacting with those outside your neighborhood, a feeling that is intensified by all the negative stories in the media. Yet, as appealing as this hospitality was, I couldn't easily replace my ingrained reflex of suspicion with trust and acceptance. I found I was always a bit worried about…about I don't know what. Just worried.

Despite the wind, it was a beautiful day for riding. Much of my route hugged the Mississippi. Visible on the side of the road were towering fifty-foot high dirt levees built up from decades of man trying to contain the river. In his book *Control of Nature*, the author John McPhee examines how the U.S. Army Corps of Engineers has attempted to control the Mississippi River for decades to promote better commerce and agriculture. But when I saw the enormous size of some of those levees and realized how frequently they were breached by storms and floods—Hurricane Katrina being the latest example—I understood that the Corps, despite its best efforts, would always be overmatched.

Reaching the town of Innis, I pulled over at a food mart to grab some lunch. As I leaned against the building, eating a sandwich and blocked from the wind, a man in a freshly pressed Louisiana State University sweatshirt approached and began excitedly peppering me with questions about my ride. Frank was in his mid-50s, short and heavy with black curly hair streaked with gray. As we spoke, he told me that he worked with the Louisiana Office of the Secretary of State and flashed a silver badge in his wallet to prove it. He was exceedingly polite and deeply interested in what I was doing, offering to help me in any way needed. But he was almost too nice, giving me the sense that at any moment he would ask if I had ever considered a beautiful little timeshare in St. Landry Parish. Feeling uneasy, I brought our conversation to a close, shook hands with him, and departed on my bike.

Forty-five minutes later, a gleaming new Chevy pickup truck slid to a halt in the gravel on the side of the road in front of me. As I slowed to a stop, Frank jumped out with his hand wrapped around a cold beer.

"Hey there. I was hopin' I'd find ya," he said as he walked toward me. "I was talkin' to some of my huntin' buddies, and we're gonna have a cookout tonight. My friend Jimmy bagged a boar, and we're gonna roast it. I told 'em about you, and they said tah give ya an invite."

"Well, thanks," I responded hesitantly. "Sounds like a good time, but I haven't put in many miles today."

"C'mon son. You should join us. It'll give you a chance to meet some REAL good ole boys," he said with a laugh.

"Appreciate the offer, but I've really got to get in some riding today. I've got a long way to go still. But thanks," I said, shaking his hand.

"Ok. Y'all stay safe," he said in a disappointed voice before walking back to his truck.

On reflection, I'm sure this type of hospitality was part of his Southern DNA, but I just didn't feel comfortable accepting the offer. It's unfair to say, but, the entire time he was speaking, I could hear "Dueling Banjos" playing in the back of my mind.

This was a constant internal conflict—my desire for exploration and adventure against my ingrained fear from years of city living that something calamitous might occur. This fear was intensified because I was travelling alone. Here was an opportunity to "take the road less traveled" and to discover what life was like in the local community and I chose safety instead of some delicious barbecued pork and the chance to meet some interesting characters. But I just couldn't shake that sense of distrust. As I watched Frank drive off, I mounted my saddle and continued down the road, all the while thinking how disappointed I was in myself.

seven

Simmesport to Opelousas, Louisiana
Total Ride Mileage: 860

While traveling through the South, I learned from personal experience that for many people, dogs are the preferred type of home security system. In this area it seemed that menacing mongrels were a feature of almost every house. Travelling the bridge-road into the town of Simmesport was like riding a canine gauntlet. I pedaled it tentatively, clinging to the centerline of the road trying to appear relaxed and confident in the face of multiple ferocious dogs charging at me. I would reflexively tense; get ready to pedal hard, and then each attack would abruptly end with a snarl and a yelp when the dog hit the limit of a rope or chain tied to its collar.

I passed one particularly aggressive looking dog on the opposite side of the road and bluffingly gave it my most insouciant glance. The animal responded with a low growl and a stare that said, "Let's get ready to rumble." Within seconds, it was streaking toward me like a hairy black and tan Tomahawk missile. I looked over my shoulder in mild alarm and waited a few moments for it to hit the end of its rope. But it didn't. This dog was untethered. Jumping onto my pedals, I began to accelerate. The dog, however, was relentless, weaving in and out of speeding cars and trucks to get at me. After a quarter-mile, it had reached within striking distance of my foot, and I pulled a stone from the back pocket of my jersey and threw it in the dog's direction. (After repeated encounters, I had overcome my reluctance to pelting aggressive dogs with rocks.) I missed, but thankfully the dog stopped to sniff the rock and I was able to escape without harm.

After catching my breath and riding a bit further, I arrived in Simmesport where I wandered around the town until I located the Yellow Bayou Civil War Memorial Park, which was advertised as a city-operated campground. "Campground" was a stretch. A big stretch. In reality, it was a run-down local park with a weed-filled children's playground that abutted the highway. No designated camping sites, no facilities, no privacy and no quiet.

Quickly, I abandoned the idea of camping and doubled back into town, locating one of the only hotels in the area, one that will forever be imprinted in my memory as "Hotel Hades." The dingy, darkened lobby and surly attitude of the desk clerk when I checked in should have been a red flag causing me to keep riding. But it was the only place in town, and I was exhausted from the long day of riding and my earlier encounter with Cujo.

Remember those black-and-white newsreels of cigarette-smoking machines used for nicotine testing in the 1960s? I'm certain they were filmed in my room. Everything looked worn, broken, and stained and reeked of smoke. The room had clearly never seen a vacuum cleaner or dust rag. I eyed the bed with apprehension, not daring to check under the blanket for fear of what lived in the sheets. Instead, I unrolled my sleeping bag on top of the bedspread.

In desperate need of a shower, I walked into the bathroom with low expectations, which were immediately met. As I looked around, I noticed missing tiles on the floor, mold covering much of the glass shower door, and a cracked mirror over the sink. The bathroom was so disgusting that the small wrapped bar of hand soap looked oddly out of place.

Stripping down, I walked under the shower and lathered up before I realized that there were no towels anywhere in the room. Assuming this was an oversight, I dressed and went back to the lobby to request some.

Walking up to the front desk in my now wet clothing, I politely said, "Excuse me, there are no towels in my room."

In response, the desk clerk exploded in rage, waving his hands wildly and raising his voice as if I had requested a pedicure and a free massage: "You people always take towels. Whatta ya need a towel for?"

"Err, I'd like to take a shower and I need one to dry off?"

"Didn't you bring one on your bike?" he asked accusingly.

"No, I didn't."

"We don't have any more."

"You run a hotel. You've got to have towels," I implored.

"No. We have none."

"I don't believe you," I said forcefully.

Finally, he turned around and stormed into a room behind the lobby, muttering angrily. A few moments later, he reappeared and shoved over a single threadbare, ripped piece of cloth and waved me away dismissively.

Thankful that I didn't need to request something more challenging like running water or electricity, I headed back to my room. After finally managing a shower, I crawled into my bag, desperate for sleep. Instead, for the next few hours, I listened to the muffled thumps and periodic yells from what was either a domestic disturbance or a drug deal gone wrong in the room next door. It was going to be a long night.

That evening turned out to be less exciting than I had feared, but I still managed little sleep. At first light, I decided to leave, stopping only at a local gas station for directions and a quick breakfast in the station mini-mart. While sipping my coffee at a small table, a man in jeans and a camouflage hunter's jacket and cap sat down across from me and introduced himself. Mark grew up in Simmesport, but had left town when he was in high school to work in a factory on the other end of the state. Five years earlier, he had injured himself and was unable to work in his manufacturing job again. He returned home and since then had been helping his father run the family farm where they grew cotton, sugar cane, wheat, rice, and beans. Mark also told me that they flooded one of their fields to raise crayfish. I discovered that in the South these crustaceans were farmed in a field like other crops.

I asked Mark about all the traffic I had seen that morning. Despite the early hour, there were a surprising number of tractors, pickups, and other agricultural vehicles on the road. He explained that the weather reports had forecast a good week for planting, and the farmers were anxious to take advantage of it. Because of the cold, wet weather that year, the planting season in the area had already been delayed for weeks. If the farmers didn't plant soon, they would be limited to one crop rather than two that season, and the economic impact to them and their community would be severe.

As I traveled across the country, this was a concern that I heard from others as well, be they fishermen, ranchers, or farmers. It wasn't described with politically charged phrases like "global warming" or "climate change;" instead people in almost every community acknowledged that the weather had been getting strange and unpredictable over the last few decades and was now casting uncertainty on their lives and livelihoods. A conversation with any septuagenarian farmer always seemed to include a description of how the regular rhythm of the seasons had disappeared since his youth. These people didn't care about measurements of CO_2 parts per million or whether the climate variation was caused by man or due to normal cyclical patterns. Instead, they were focused on something more immediate—would the weather that season allow them to support their families?

After we finished our coffee, Mark took a look at my map and planned route. He suggested that I take a different road, one that ran along the levee and continued through St. Landry Parish, the towns of Palmetto, Lebeau, and Washington and into the heart of what was known as "Cajun Country." Following his recommendation, I travelled for miles on rolling country roads lined with small, well-kept family farms.

In short, it was idyllic. I felt as if I were riding through a 1960s-era Disney movie. Just as I was getting ready to start singing a duet with a little cartoon bluebird, I turned a bend and saw four dogs jump off the porch of a rickety old house a few hundred feet from the road and tear toward me. Adrenaline flooded my bloodstream. I launched up in my pedals and started pumping. By the time I passed the dogs, they had narrowed the distance considerably. Looking over my shoulder, I could see their owner, a bearded, ancient-looking man, stomping on the porch and yelling. But he had such a thick Cajun accent that I couldn't understand if he was urging the dogs to stop or imploring them to go for my calves. Like a steam locomotive pulling a line of boxcars, it took me time to get up to full speed, but once I did, the dogs tired and at last dropped off behind me. To be certain that I was out of their range, I continued for another half-mile before pulling over, leaning on the handlebars, and gasping for breath as I waited for my body to stop shaking.

Thirty minutes later, the same thing happened again. This time it was a small terrier that was interested in a bit of Mike meat for lunch. When I first caught sight of the dog it was chasing me from behind a wooden picket fence, so I gave it little attention. A few moments later, I realized that the gate was open. Again, there was another lengthy sprint before this fellow also gave up.

The dogs of the South were really getting to me. A random bark in the distance would raise my pulse. The sight of a man walking a dog on a leash would quicken my breathing. Even seeing a poster in a pet shop window seeking the return of some child's lost border collie would instantly cause me to quiver.

For several decades, I'd been addicted to coffee. I generally downed four to six cups each morning, a byproduct of life in the corporate world. I knew that I'd had enough when I started shaking. A goal for this ride was to kick the habit, but my need for morning warmth and energy made this impossible. As I pedaled, I thought that when I got home, the menacing dogs of St. Landry Parish might be the answer. It would work like this:

Setting: breakfast table at home.

Liz: "Good morning, honey. Do you want coffee or canines this morning?"

Me: "Better go with the dogs today."

Liz: "Really? Did you have a bad night's sleep?"

Me: "Terrible. I was tossing all night."

Liz gives me a kiss, slips some headphones over my ears, and asks: "Do you want the tan and white pit bull?"

Me: "No, better make it the Doberman mix followed by the feral terrier."

Liz: "Wow, you really did have a terrible night!" She then hits the play button and watches my face flush, my pupils dilate, and a light perspiration coat my forehead while I listen to the sound of attacking canines.

Me: "Thanks, honey. Wide awake now and ready for work."

As you can see, the mind really wanders when you are alone on a long ride.

eight

Opelousas to DeRidder, Louisiana
Total Ride Mileage: 946

On most days I found my attention drawn to the subtle changes in my sur-roundings. The slow, methodical cadence of my wheels heightened my focus on the details of what surrounded me: a mailbox welded together out of rusted tractor parts, the curious pattern on a cow's hide, the mesmeric design of a freshly plowed field. Often, however, it was just mind-numbing hours of pedal-ing with little visual distraction. During these times, the three-inch white line on the edge of the roadway became a rail that I stared at while silently begging for the miles to disappear.

Maybe it was my Zen-like focus on the line. Perhaps it was just boredom, but on these days my attention turned inward and for hours I swam deeply in a pool of self-doubt. Was I the man I wanted to be? The husband my wife deserved? Would my children be proud of me as they grew older? Did I spend enough time honoring my parents for all they had provided? Did others truly value my friendship? Had I done enough to help colleagues be successful in their careers? Was my own career finally over? For miles I would drown myself in these anxieties and uncertainties, questioning who I was. Until at some point, I would finally say "enough," press harder on the pedals, and silently vow to do better when I returned home.

Riding to Oberlin was one of those days. With little to note in the scenery, or from my emotional self-flagellation, I wrote only this haiku in my journal before I went to sleep that evening:

Today wind at back
Rode Mamou to Oberlin
Went too fast for dogs

As I traveled, I had become almost "Pirsig" in my approach to maintaining my bike and packing my gear. Each morning, I applied what I learned from my college reading of *Zen and the Art of Motorcycle Maintenance*. I'd check the brakes and derailleur and then run my fingers across each spoke like a harpist tuning his instrument, listening for any that were loose. Next, I would spin the wheels to check their alignment and look for spots of wear on the tires. I would follow this by giving the frame a vigorous shake to see if anything was loose and rattled. Finally, I repacked each pannier with exactly the same gear so that I could effortlessly locate items. I rarely found any problems of note, but this small daily discipline provided a measure of comfort to the uncertainty of each day.

After finishing my mechanical check early the next morning, I rode through downtown Oberlin, looking for a place for breakfast. Nothing appeared open until I reached the outskirts of town. There I found "Keith's Corner," an aggregation of commercial enterprises, including a grocery store, café, and large car wash. Evidently, Keith was Oberlin's version of Donald Trump.

Stopping in front of the café, I leaned my bike against a post and pulled out two of my three cable locks. Having my bike and gear stolen and being stranded in some remote southern town was a constant worry. As I went to lock the bike, I noticed a woman leaning against a nearby post taking a deep drag from a cigarette and staring at me. She had stringy blonde hair, a pocked complexion, and an emaciated body that looked straight out of a TV public service announcement about the dangers of meth addiction. In a raspy voice she slowly said, "Honey, y'all don't need to worry about lockin' your bike. Nobody's gonna steal it 'round here. If they do we just shoot 'em.'"

I looked at her and laughed, but her face didn't reveal even the suggestion of a smile as she started at me and continued puffing. Feeling uncomfortable, but not wanting to offend her, I nodded and reluctantly returned my locks to the panniers.

As I opened the door to the windowless café, I was instantly hit by a blast of hot, greasy air. My glasses fogged with an oily film as I stepped to the counter and ordered a BLT, hashed browns, and a ham and cheese omelet, and poured myself a mug of scalding coffee. As I did, a white-haired man with large-framed glasses and a Mr. Rogers-style sweater beckoned me to a table where he was sitting with a cup of coffee.

"Name's Jim. Where are you headed, son?" he said as he shook my hand.

"Ultimately, I'm heading home, which is south of San Francisco."

He nodded and asked, "Have you ever heard of Chico, California?"

"Sure, I've been there a few times."

"I was born and raised in Chico!" He exclaimed.

And with that, Jim began to tell me the story of his life, continuing on without pause for the next hour while I enjoyed my coffee and breakfast across the table from him.

When he was a young man, Jim fell in love with a local Oberlin girl he had met during World War II. He followed his heart and moved from California to Oberlin to marry her. Along the way, he and his wife raised a family and, for 45 years, he served as the town's only pharmacist. Since his retirement twenty years earlier (Jim was in his late 80s), he had been coming to this café almost every morning and holding court. This was apparent from the playful banter between him and the waitresses, which would have made for a well-practiced 1960s Catskills comedy show.

"They all know me here," he said, waving a bony finger at the waitresses, one of whom acknowledged Jim's statement with a roll of her eyes and a teasing smile.

Jim proved to be a seemingly inexhaustible source of information. When I mentioned how the scenery seemed to be changing from crayfish farms to forests, he gave me a tutorial on pine trees, one of the major crops in the area.

"The tree of choice 'round here is the loblolly pine. Funny sounding name, isn't it? It grows quickly in our climate and, most importantly, straight," he said.

"What are they used for?"

"A variety of things. Farmers plant about 1,000 trees per acre and harvest a portion of them each decade. Trees at 10 years are milled for garden stakes, at 20 years they're used for furniture, and at 30 years for telephone poles and paper products. The sawdust is even used for a bunch of stuff."

From there Jim changed subjects and began educating me on Oberlin's economy, history, and infrastructure. As he did, Grady, the town's chief of police, arrived. Jim introduced us, and Grady and I ate breakfast together, exchanging grins and raised eyebrows as Jim expounded without pause on a broad array of subjects. In that moment, I had the feeling that many locals had shared my same experience listening to Jim every morning for years.

It felt comfortable to spend time with Jim, to enjoy this brief bit of companionship and hold my loneliness at bay. Jim must have felt the same or was appreciative of having an audience for he was clearly disappointed when I finally finished eating and told him it was time for me to leave. As I shook hands with him and Grady, I felt as if I were stepping out of an American archetype: locals "chewing the fat" over an early morning breakfast. However, my thoughts became more grounded in reality as I headed out the door wondering if I would be returning to report a stolen bicycle to Grady. To my relief, I found it untouched.

After leaving Oberlin, I rode for thirty minutes before I was flagged down by a rider traveling in the opposite direction. He was a large dour-looking man, dressed from head to toe in worn brown camouflage, with a long, unkempt Fu Manchu-style mustache. His mountain bike was decrepit. In a gravelly voice, he asked if I knew anything about bicycles because his was struggling to change gears. I took a look at his chain and saw that it was almost rusted solid. Flipping the bike over, I pulled some lubricant from the pocket of my pannier and soaked the links. After a few minutes of working the pedals and levers, things started to loosen, and I was able to shift into some additional gears. Then I flipped the bike back over, handed it to him, and said: "This should be a bit better." In response, he surprised me by giving me a big bear hug and jumping up and down like a contestant on *Wheel of Fortune*. I said "no problem" and pedaled away thinking about the kind people I had met on the road and appreciating how little it sometimes takes to help someone out.

For the next 25 miles I journeyed along pine tree farms that were just as Jim had described. The day's mileage was my shortest to date, but I had decided to make the town of DeRidder my destination for the night. One of the lessons I was learning was to avoid the "Sirens of the Road" (a term coined by Don). This referred to a state of mind experienced by many touring cyclists on long distance rides. You roll into a location that has a nice campsite or motel, but it is still early in the afternoon. You feel strong and want to get in some additional miles. The Sirens seductively beckon to you to keep riding. You submit to the temptation and follow, and the next thing you know, the sun has set, you're in the middle of nowhere, and you can't a find a decent place to stay for the evening. I had experienced this several times during the previous weeks. In one case, I had seriously considered sleeping in a stack of concrete sewage tubes near a construction site, but thoughts of snakes and spiders motivated me to keep moving until I finally found a motel after riding many miles farther in the dark.

With experience, however, comes wisdom (or else fulfillment of Darwin's theory of natural selection). Although plenty of daylight remained, I forced myself to stop outside of DeRidder at a place known as Pleasant Hill RV and Campground.

As campgrounds go, it wasn't particularly attractive. It consisted of little more than 10 sites for car and tent camping situated under a cluster of pine trees at the edge of a housing tract. Yet Pleasant Hill was legendary among cyclists in the southern U.S. because of its caretakers, "Miss Pat" and her late husband, who had catered to touring cyclists for years. For $5 I had access to a laundry, shower, kitchen, and communal living room lined with books, maps, and guest logs. It felt almost decadent compared to some of my recent accommodations.

While setting up camp next to the picnic table in my assigned area, I met Jan and Irene, two women in their early sixties who hailed from Michigan. I noticed on the back of their van a touring bicycle with a handlebar basket filled with an assortment of small stuffed animals. When I asked about it, Jan replied that she had named the bike "Esmerelda" and that she was riding it across the country. The stuffed animals in the basket kept her company on lonely stretches of highway. Like me, she had started in Florida, but was averaging 30-40 miles per day. According to their daily routine, Irene would pick up Jan when she was done with her day's ride and transport her and Esmerelda to a pre-arranged hotel or campground for the evening. Then, the next morning Irene would return Jan to her finishing point of the previous day where she would begin again. While Jan was riding, Irene was exploring a broader swath of the country from the seat of her van and doing less strenuous sightseeing.

Irene's van was loaded with gear, including sleeping bags, lawn chairs, tennis racquets, and even two sewing machines so that she and Jan could sew quilts at their campground each evening. It was clear that Jan and Irene had been friends for many years. They not only sewed together, but finished each other's sentences, laughed at each other's jokes, and gently teased one another whenever the opportunity arose.

After weeks of travelling many of the same roads, the three of us enjoyed a night of lively conversation, the kind that occurs between strangers who find they have a unique shared experience. As we talked, I thought about the distance I had covered. The following day I would cross into Texas. Almost in spite of the inclement weather, the dogs, and the gloomy pall of Katrina, I had enjoyed my time in the Deep South. But now I was beginning to feel the gentle pull of the West. Of the eight states I would traverse on my ride, Texas was the one that caused me the most apprehension. Given its reputation for political and social conservatism, its identity as a major part of the Bible Belt and its embrace of personal firearms, I knew that I would feel like an outsider.

Plus, it was a big-ass state to cross on a bicycle.

Section 3

Continuing His Journey, Our Hero Encounters the Great State of
Texas and Learns About Javelinas, the Bible Belt,
and the Pleasures of Lone Star Beer.

(Texas)

nine

DeRidder, Louisiana, to Cold Spring, Texas
Total Ride Mileage: 1,091

As I rode through Beauregard Parish the following morning, I could sense a change. The landscape was drier and filled almost exclusively with pines; the palmettos of the South were falling behind. Along one desolate highway, thousands of FEMA trailers stretched in rows to the horizon, all staged and solemnly awaiting the next hurricane, tornado, or other natural calamity. As I traced the curves of the road, trucks stacked with pine logs and wood chips rushed past me heading for a local mill. Winding through the delightfully named town of Merryville, I crossed the Sabine River and suddenly I was in the Lone Star State.

A few miles past the state line, I came upon a road construction site with front loaders and dump trucks blocking the highway. A flagman signaled me to stop and, seeing my sweat-soaked jersey, said: "Son, you look like you need a break. This is a good excuse." He noticed my panniers and asked where I was heading. When I explained, he stuck out his heavily calloused hand to shake mine and with a big smile said: "Well, sir, my name is Jeff Franklin. Welcome to Texas!" Then he reached into his waistband to show me a crucifix and his Colt Defender .45 handgun. (OK, maybe I made up that last part.)

Before waving me ahead, Jeff mentioned a rider who had passed by a short time earlier. By the description I knew it was Don. After a few minutes of high speed pedaling, I caught up with him, and we pulled over to the side of the road for a brief reunion before riding the remaining 35 miles into the town of Silsbee. I'm not sure whether it was the desire for a hot shower or some long dormant spirit of competition, but Don and I raced the remaining distance and were both completely drained by the time we reached the Red Cloud RV Park in Silsbee.

When we arrived and checked in, the camp host directed us a few hundred feet from the nearest motor home to a shadeless lawn abutting the noisy highway as the location for us to set up our gear. In the camping caste system, it was clear that cyclists were considered worthy of sites far below motor homes and car campers and closer to places where one's pets might relieve themselves. But, I was too tired to care.

As Don and I were setting up camp, a cyclist arrived from the west, pulling a trailer behind a recumbent bicycle. Before he fully slowed to a stop, he looked at us and began a Yosemite Sam obscenity-laced description of the flat tires, aggressive drivers, poor roads, and adverse weather that he had faced through western Texas. Erwin was a 75-year-old grandfather of two. He had left his family a couple of months earlier and started his ride in San Diego. He was now on his way home to North Carolina. Fatigue and years lined his face, and it took several minutes before he had the strength to lift himself from his seat and an even longer time before he slowly started pulling together his equipment for the night.

At about this same time, I was surprised when Jan and Irene, whom I had met a day earlier in DeRidder, pulled into the same campsite. I could tell from her face that Jan was tired from her day of riding Esmerelda with her basket of stuffed animals. Erwin was clearly wiped out as well and Don was already taking a nap in his tent.

The serendipity of four cyclists in the same campsite was worth celebrating, but none of us had the energy to cook. Instead, we later crammed into Irene's van amidst the camping gear and sewing machines and drove to the first barbecue joint we found off the highway. Over dinner, we tried to muster the energy to compare experiences. But full stomachs, cold Lone Star beer, and fatigue left us unable to share more than a few solitary sentences. Even Don was unable to utter more than a few words, and those were limited to synonyms for the word "exhausted."

We returned to camp in the early evening, exchanged our goodnights, and burrowed into our sleeping bags. Given my fatigue, I had hoped for a deep and full night's slumber. It was not to be, for this was St. Patrick's Day, and evidently Texas karaoke bars such as the one adjacent to the campground celebrated the

occasion with gusto. Not even earplugs could muffle the music, drunken singing, and slamming car doors of each new patron arriving at the bar throughout
the night.

The following day I packed and departed before my fellow riders were awake.
I continued through a series of small, undistinguished towns with names like
Kountze, Honey Island, Thicket, Votaw, Rye, Romayor, Dolen, Shepherd,
and Coldspring. (By the way, this list sounds better with Johnny Cash's song
"I've Been Everywhere" running through your head as you read it.) For long
distances, the road was deserted. After weeks of riding through a range of
road conditions, I was gradually gaining an increasing connectedness with my
bicycle. I could feel when the tires needed a few more pounds of air pressure
and sensed when I had slightly more weight in one pannier than the others.
My confidence was growing. Rather than worrying about what was coming up
behind me on the road, I had begun to think about what was ahead.

Tentatively, I edged from the shoulder, over the solid white line, and into
the car lane. After I pedaled there for a few miles, the empty roadway beckoned
me to the middle and then, almost without thought, I was snaking in and out of
the dashed center line like I did as a kid on my Schwinn Stingray. I was finding
youth in the miles.

It was the first day in three weeks that I had not seen any Mardi Gras
beads. Since Tallahassee, I had spotted them on highways and county roads,
everywhere and in every color— tangerine, lavender, black, white, turquoise—a
constant reminder of the Southern spirit of "Laissez les bon temps rouler." At
times they were so plentiful that it seemed as though an errant Mardi Gras float
had gone off course and was traveling ahead of me. Now the beads were gone
and replaced by the small circular dirt rings built by mudbugs (a relative of the
crayfish) dotting the roadside as the South disappeared behind me.

In the late afternoon, I pulled over at a small liquor store for a snack and
a carton of chocolate milk. The clerk, an irascible older gentleman with a grizzled white beard and obviously little concern about his missing dentures, tried
to convince me that I should drink a few beers as I pedaled to help give me

energy. He then shifted into an angry rant about changes to Texas laws that prohibited driving with an open container, pointing out that when he was a youth he would drive with a bottle of Jack Daniel's between his legs. He then launched into a scholarly dissection of the current law and provided an analysis worthy of a constitutional law scholar of why it shouldn't apply to a man riding a bicycle. To humor him (really, that's the only reason), I also bought a 20-oz. can of Budweiser and, after I left the store, stashed it in my pannier for later in the evening.

The conditions were perfect for riding—minimal winds, smooth pavement, and a sunny day. But I was exhausted when I at last I settled into the campground that evening. After more than 1,000 miles, my body felt like it was nothing more than a collection of bruised muscles and aching joints. Recently, I'd started to develop a strange numbness in my left hand, almost as if my palm and fingers were constantly asleep. My right knee was also giving me problems. Toward the end of each day's ride, I felt a "clicking" sensation when I pedaled, and my knee throbbed as I tried to sleep at night. The physical pain was made worse by my growing concern that an injury might bring an early end to my trip. I tried to put these worries out of mind. In less than a week I would be in Austin and could give myself time to heal under Liz's tender care. Our daughter, Emily, was a synchronized swimmer and she and Liz would be in Austin for a few days for a competition.

The thought of being with them was salve to my sore joints and muscles and lightened my spirit.

ten

Cold Spring to Giddings, Texas
Total Ride Mileage: 1,236

For urbanites, the sparseness of the West can be jarring. An entire town may have a population of less than a city high school. A trip to the store is measured in miles, not blocks. And sitting quietly on the porch is a valued form of recreation. The following day I absorbed all of this as I again wove through a repetition of small towns. In some, the Texas flag over the city hall was almost larger than the downtown area.

I stopped at a convenience store in one of these towns. As I leaned my bicycle against the glass door, I noticed the clerk, a young woman, looking at me.

When I placed a bottle of water on the counter to purchase, she said, "Saw ya ridin' your bike. Where ya headed?"

"I'm on my way home to California."

"California! Oh, my gosh, I've always dreamed of goin' to California," she said wistfully.

"Why don't you?"

"Don't I what?"

"Go to California."

"Ah, I could never do that. I went to school here. My family is here. This is my home." She paused and then said with a sigh: "I'll be here forever."

I thought about her as I mounted my bike and rode off. Her response was similar to what I had heard from others over the past weeks when I mentioned where I lived. To them, California wasn't just a state, but a state of mind. People spoke of it in almost reverential terms, as if it were some mystical place. I always found this a bit strange. Why not just drive west and find a job there? Or at least visit? What was keeping her in this small Texas town? Was it really her family or was it the fear of failure that comes when following a dream? I'm not sure, but listening to her voice it was clear that there was something that would never let her bridge that distance.

As I travelled through eastern Texas, the most prevalent scenery—aside from livestock and landscape—continued to be churches. The Mardi Gras beads may have been gone, but the presence of the Bible Belt intensified. For amusement, I switched from counting road kill and began to keep a churches-per-mile tally. In my first 30 miles of riding that morning, I counted 26 of them, almost as many as the number of homes I saw in the area. They ranged from small one-room clapboard structures to mega-churches with electronic Jumbotron-style screens. Each used a sign in front as a form of salvation marketing.

The Tabernacle Church of Christ, for example, used a direct but poetic message:

"Life is short. Death is sure. Sin is the curse, but Christ is the cure."

The Warrington Assembly of God attempted a sports metaphor:

"Life is like tennis, serve well and you seldom lose."

While the New Life Fellowship Assembly of God tried for a more succinct and cheerful entreaty:

"Smile, God loves you."

The only thing I saw more often than churches in the area were billboards advertising personal injury attorneys. I wasn't sure what these two things said about the South, but somewhere in there was an interesting PhD dissertation for a sociology student.

Most disconcerting about the Bible Belt, however, was not the omnipresence of the churches, but rather the abdication of personal responsibility that I heard from some of the local parishioners. The phrase "It's God's will" came up more often in conversations than was comfortable for me.

One evening, I spent time speaking with a camp host, a woman in her early thirties. Her husband was a pipefitter who was away working on a project for a few days. While I cooked dinner in the communal kitchen, she joined me along with her precocious four-year-old daughter. This little girl was fascinating to watch: creative, curious, and bright with an advanced vocabulary. As I prepared my meal, I listened to the woman's story. She was a high school dropout who as a teenager married a much older man and had several unplanned pregnancies, children, and an early divorce. She later remarried, a marriage that had resulted in the little girl playing beside us. The woman described a sad life of failed jobs, substance abuse problems, and years drifting around the country. I tried to turn the conversation in a more positive direction by commenting on the woman's amazing daughter and asking about her plans for the child. Where did she want her daughter to go to school? What was she doing to enhance the girl's already impressive abilities? What did she want for her daughter's life? To each of my questions, I received a vague and shallow response along with a recitation that her daughter's life would ultimately be up to "God's will."

Listening to her reply, I sensed that the woman had given little serious thought to the future of her daughter. Perhaps I was just run-down and feeling overly pessimistic, but when I looked at this delightful little girl playing at the end of the table, I wondered if she was destined to follow the same life as her mother.

For a large part of the next day, I travelled through Sam Houston National Forest and around Lake Livingston through dense corridors of pines. The countryside was providing whispers of the West. Agave and prickly pear cacti sporadically appeared. Farms were giving way to ranches. And the influences of Cajun and African American culture were shifting to Hispanic. For me, this meant an enormous repast at a local taqueria after I checked into my motel in Navasota for the evening. It was glorious. I downed a plate of beef tacos smothered in guacamole and sour cream, an order of chile relleno, and two margaritas. In a single meal I did my best to replenish all the calories I had burned in the entire day.

I awoke the next morning to the first day of spring, but the weather failed to note the calendar. With heavy, slate gray skies overhead, I rode through downtown Navasota in search of a cup of coffee at a nearby doughnut shop. After I ordered from the waitress, I struck up a conversation with an older local ranch hand seated in the booth opposite me. His battered Levi's jacket, large frame and weathered face reflected a lifetime managing ranches throughout eastern and central Texas. Belying his hardened appearance, he surprised me with an extensive knowledge of local wildflowers.

"You just headin' through?" he asked.

"Yep. Not sure about the weather today, but the scenery is wonderful. Don't think I've ever seen so many wildflowers."

"Most of the one's you see 'round here are primrose. But you can also find some poppies, coneflowers and firewheels. Some folks also call them Indian blanket. They're the ones that have little pink flowers with yellow points."

Then, in the midst of his description of Texas bluebonnets, a cornea-melting flash filled the shop, followed by a jarring explosion that launched me off my seat causing me to spill my coffee. Was it a bomb? Had a plane crashed? As I turned to look out the window, still pulsing with adrenaline, I heard him say in a slow, understated baritone drawl: "Looks like we're havin' a bit of weather today."

Then the rain started. Within moments the road and parking lot were inches deep in water, and it was clear that I wasn't going anywhere. For the next hour the thunder roared with concussive power in combination with a mesmerizing display of lightning. While dunking my glazed in a cup of coffee, I watched the light show and thought: There's nothing like a Texas storm to give you a sense of your place in the natural world.

The following day the Sirens of the Road destroyed me. After waiting out the storm in Navasota, I got up the next morning and checked the weather report for the day. Frost warnings had been issued with temperatures predicted to reach no higher than the low 40s. I dressed in all my riding clothes, including long gloves, a wool cap, wool turtleneck, thermal vest, windbreaker, wool leggings, and rain pants—and still never felt warm once during the day.

As I headed toward the town of Brenham, two riders pedaling toward me on the opposite side of the road pulled over to talk. They were a retired couple from Quebec. We huddled close together to block the wind as we quickly spoke about where we were riding. They had started in San Diego and were heading to Florida. They told me that they were going to do a short ride that day, less than 25 miles, because the temperature was too cold for them. When someone from Quebec complains about the cold, you know it's real.

For the following hours that morning I rode into a wind that escalated in ferocity, causing my nylon rain pants to snap and crack loudly with every gust. It was, in short, a frigid, interminable grind. A few miles outside of Brenham, a hand-lettered sign in front of a ranch-style house advertised "home style" barbecue. The adjacent dirt parking lot was filled with well-used cars and tired pickup trucks. Coasting to a stop, I decided to use a pulled pork sandwich as an opportunity to get warm and out of the wind.

The large dining room was filled with people sitting at picnic tables covered with plastic red-checkered tablecloths, and ordering food from a kitchen countertop. They instantly greeted me like a momentary celebrity: "Thought you'd never make it up that last hill," "That wind near blow'd ya over back there," "What the hell ya doin' on a bike in this weather, boy?" Evidently, they all had passed me on their way to lunch and I had become the local entertainment.

After finishing my sandwich and reviving a bit, I left and continued riding on in the wind, until a short while later I reached Brenham. It was a town with history—Texas signed its Declaration of Independence from Mexico nearby— and a charming downtown with century-old restored buildings and several small, inviting hotels. In short, it was the type of place where I normally would have been inclined to spend a night. But I was feeling strong and warmed by the physical exertion, and I listened to the Sirens who whispered convincingly that I could make it to Giddings—another 40 miles.

It was a terrible decision.

The wind nearly overpowered me as I rode out of Brenham and headed into the Texas Hill Country hunched over my handlebar drops. A quirky yet endearing feature of my bicycle was that the builder, Bruce Gordon, placed a small decal of a golden rooster on the middle of the handle bar stem on each bike he built. It etched itself in my brain; with my head down against the unrelenting wind, I used the decal as a focal point while trying to keep the bike upright. Several times I stopped under an overpass or in some other sheltered area to try to regain warmth and think of another option. There wasn't one. I was miles from any motel or place to camp.

Exhausted and aching, I stopped when I saw a gas station mini-mart near what was identified on my map as the town of Carmine, although it was little more than an intersection with a handful of buildings. Walking along the aisles, I came upon a large plastic table in the back of the store around which were seated eight dusty, mustached, leathery-looking men dressed in worn denim work shirts, cowboy hats, and boots. Through sepia-toned eyes, you would have thought they were from an earlier century. Instead, they were drinking bottled beer, eating a pre-heated pizza, and watching the NCAA basketball finals on a large plasma TV screen. Evidently, in these parts, the local mini-mart had become the general store of the past.

It was difficult to believe, but the wind had increased by the time I was back on the road. All I could do was keep moving forward a few yards at a time at no more than five to six miles per hour. I was at the full limit of my endurance and began thinking about how selfish this all seemed. What was I trying to prove? I was an out-of-shape, middle-aged father of three, half a continent from friends and family. What in the hell was I doing? Why was I here? Above all, wasn't there any kind soul who would pull over and offer me a warm bed or at least a ride? But there was no one. I was alone and needed to finish the day on my own. I continued, moving into the wall of wind slowly and methodically, mile by mile, trying to ignore it and my self-doubt. Finally, a little after dusk, I saw the Giddings town water tower silhouetted against the western sky a few miles ahead on the horizon.

I checked into the first motel I found and collapsed asleep on the bed without even taking off my clothes.

eleven

Giddings to Austin, Texas
Total Ride Mileage: 1,293

It's amazing what 10 hours of sleep and a windless, sunny, 70-degree day will do for your spirits. After leaving Giddings the next morning, I travelled through Bastrop County, which was enveloped in carpets of wildflowers on sun-blazed hillsides—bluebonnets, Texas paintbrush, and square-bud primrose. Raptors were my constant companion. I'd never seen as many in a single day. Hawks of all kinds—red-tailed, red-shouldered, Swainson's, and several I couldn't identify—dove across the roadway. Around the base of a large oak tree, I counted 17 black vultures feasting on the carcass of a deer. They raised their heads in my direction as I passed, but thankfully didn't follow.

The beauty of my surroundings faded as I passed the town of Elgin and drew closer to Austin, where the landscape increasingly reflected the impact of urbanization. Roadside trash, fast food restaurants, gas stations, tractor sales lots, and junkyards became more frequent. But they didn't diminish my ebullience because I would soon be with my wife and daughter. The anticipation of seeing them made the remaining miles to Austin feel effortless.

Austin has always been an intersection of diverse cultures. Originally populated by Comanche and Apache Indian tribes, the area's residents expanded when the Spanish arrived to build their missions. They were in turn followed in the

1820s by a few hundred Anglo-American families, referred to in Texas lore as the "Old Three Hundred," who founded a colony and later named it for their leader, Stephen F. Austin. In the following decades, a stream of immigrants, among them Germans, Swiss, Austrians, and Prussians, began to arrive, as well as an increasing number of black Americans as slave owners moved to Texas from the battle-scarred areas of the Civil War South. This pace of immigration increased as the area's economic base shifted from farming to cattle to oil to technology.

In the last decade, Austin had become a cultural mosaic known for the music, art, and food representative of its latest group of immigrants: the 21st-century hipster. As I explored Austin, they were ubiquitous and easy to spot by their skinny jeans, vintage plaid shirts, heavy-rimmed black frame glasses, Chuck Taylor high top sneakers, and favorite accessory: a cup of any beverage made from the seeds of the coffee plant.

My first task after arriving and checking into my hotel was a visit to Mellow Johnny's bike shop as my front wheel had a wobble and needed to be trued and I wanted to replace my chain, which had become badly worn. In keeping with the influence of the area's latest group of immigrants, the shop included a nice coffee bar. I availed myself of a cappuccino as I explained to the mechanic on duty what I needed done. Unfortunately, he told me he was booked with service orders and would not be able to get to my repairs until the following week. I couldn't wait that long having planned for only a few days in Austin. Noticing that I was riding a touring bike he asked if I was planning to take a long ride. I used it as my chance to describe my travels, planned route and time constraints. In response he smiled, looked down at his computer screen, and told me that he "just found an opening" and would find a way to get the work done for me by the next day.

Leaving the bike shop, I started my wanderings around Austin by heading toward the South Congress or "SoCo" part of the city. As I did, I passed the decommissioned Stenholm power plant. Built immediately after WWII, this facility at one time provided all of the electricity for Austin. Although now abandoned, it was still striking not only for the Art Deco-style of the building, but also for the modern looking "Austin Power" signage in front. Behind a warped and rusted chain link fence, it conveyed the promise of the future from the distant past (and also a potential location for the next Mike Myers movie).

SoCo was just cool. There is really no other way to put it. The hipster crowd had clearly made this area their locus. Eclectic shops offered everything from New Age art to antiques and curios to hand-tooled cowboy boots. Silver Airstream trailers restored as mobile restaurants offering barbecue ribs, Mexican, Indian, Vietnamese food, and even cupcakes filled every parking lot.

From past travels I had learned that a good way to get an inside view on what's happening in a community was to visit a barbershop. In Austin, I discovered Avenue Barbershop ("since 1933"). The décor of the place made me feel as though I had stepped back in time, and the barbers, dressed in starched white coats, offered an "old school" cut complete with straight edge, hand-whipped foam, and talc-powdered brushes. What was striking, however, was that these were not septuagenarians, but pierced and tattooed 20- to 30-year-olds who aimed to provide barbering services as had been done in this shop for the last 80 years. I luxuriated in a shave and haircut as my barber described his favorite bars, rib joints, and the latest music from the recent South by Southwest festival held in Austin each year.

Advertisements offered more insight into the city. I saw numerous signs urging people to "Keep Austin Weird." One café had a billboard that said: "Sorry, We're Open." Little Woodrow's bar advertised: "Come early, stay late and remember nothing." It was clear that this was a city that didn't take itself too seriously.

It was also a community where all forms of art were integrated into the urban landscape. Around every corner I would hear music or view a mural or sculpture; buildings were restored to carry forward interesting architectural elements from decades past, and everywhere the air was filled with the aroma of a mouthwatering diversity of food. Portland, Santa Fe and San Francisco were other places that imbue this fusion of aesthetic and community. I wondered, why doesn't every city? With the exception of the small town of St. Francisville, I hadn't experienced anything else like it on my ride.

In the late afternoon, I visited Barton Springs. Located in the center of the city, it's a naturally fed spring with a year-round temperature of 68-70 degrees, creating a limestone pool almost an eighth of a mile long. To many Austin citizens, this is the true heart of the city. While enjoying some sun after a brief swim, I spoke to a man putting on scuba equipment nearby. It turned out that he was the city biologist and was in the process of doing a monthly count of a species of protected newts that inhabit Barton Springs. A city with its own biologist? Austin just kept getting better.

Early in the evening, after enjoying a tasty plate of ribs at Stubb's, the legendary music and barbecue restaurant, I walked to the southern edge of the Congress Avenue Bridge (now known as the Ann W. Richards Congress Ave. Bridge) and stood with a few dozen others. To the uninitiated, we would have looked like tourists watching the sunset. However, shortly after dusk, the real show began when a stream of Mexican free-tailed bats flew out from under the bridge, looking like a dark shoelace unwinding across the twilight sky. This was a nightly occurrence in Austin and a popular attraction throughout the year. Tens of thousands of bats flew that evening, but in the summer their population swells to more than a million and consumes a staggering 10,000 to 30,000 pounds of insects each evening from the skies over the city.

Heading back to my hotel for the night, I strolled along Sixth Street with its raucous bars and live entertainment; it reminded me of New Orleans' famous Bourbon Street. Even the street people embraced the energy and mirth of the area. A young panhandler walked up to me holding a collection cup and a grimy sign that read, "Smile, if you masturbate." Once I finally stopped laughing, I gave him a few bucks. Was this really Texas?

The next day, Liz arrived and still recognized me despite my cyclist's tan and loss of a few pounds. After a warm reunion, we drove to the University of Texas to watch Emily and her team compete. Now, all of you flabby, beer-swillin', former-high-school-athlete American males may want to challenge me on this, but, without doubt, synchronized swimming is one of the most grueling athletic endeavors on the planet. Trust me on this because I was once one of you, one of those guys who believed that football, baseball, and basketball players were the world's best conditioned athletes.

Synchronized swimmers train for ridiculous amounts of time both in the pool and in the weight room. As a result, they develop a balance of endurance, finesse, and strength, and the lung capacity of a large sperm whale. Because synchronized swimmers spend so much energy holding their breath during underwater drills it is not uncommon for them to pass out and sink to the pool bottom, only to be rescued by an attentive teammate or coach.

My appreciation for the fitness level of the sport began when my daughter was 13 and had been in synchronized swimming for five years. As a former speed swimmer myself, I thought I'd take her to the pool to teach her about distance swimming, believing that synchronized swimmers only had the ability to effectively cover short distances. With my daughter in the next lane, I cautioned her to take it easy and pace herself because the distance we would be covering, a mile, would be long for her. We put on our goggles and started swimming; quickly, I was in my zone. Stroke, stroke, stroke, breath, stroke, stroke, stroke, and flip turn. I had covered a bit more than half a mile when I approached the wall, readied for a turn—and felt a hand on my back. It was Emily leaning against the side of the pool.

"Dad," she said. "Is it OK if I keep going?"

"What do you mean 'keep going'?" I asked.

"I finished the mile and still feel like swimming. Is that OK?"

Now, after three days of watching the competition from the poolside bleachers, Liz and I saw Emily step onto the podium to receive a medal. She had placed first in her event. I couldn't help but be filled with pride knowing what she had endured to get there—the long, lonely hours swimming laps, the nagging injuries, the exhaustion, the training in all types of weather. Unexpectedly, I found myself quietly sobbing, overcome by emotion. Surreptitiously wiping my eyes, I thought about all that my daughter had achieved. These thoughts quickly transformed into thoughts about my own journey and the emotional and physical distance I had travelled since leaving Florida; above all, I realized how much I missed my family. At that moment, if Liz had asked me to return home with them, it would have been almost impossible to refuse.

Thankfully, she didn't, and after congratulations and farewells to Emily and her teammates, Liz and I enjoyed a last dinner together and returned to our hotel, where we caught up on last-minute family details while I readied my bicycle for the remainder of the ride. Something had changed in me over the past 1,300 miles. As I packed my panniers, I thought back to when I was planning this trip earlier in the year. My focus then was on motion, on doing something, on seeking an outlet with no real certainty whether I would actually complete the ride. Now, with the miles I had travelled, I felt a growing confidence that I could finish the more than 1,200 miles to home.

I decided to lighten my load as I did some final packing the following morning. Much of my cold weather gear, a few spare tubes, an extra tire pump, and the three cable locks I had been carrying were packed into Liz's suitcase.

Then, after eating a quick breakfast together and running out of excuses to delay, I gave my lovely wife a final embrace, and I was off.

Austin was a difficult place to leave. The food, music, and art were captivating, and the barbecue sauce exuding from my pores was a reminder of how much I had enjoyed myself. But the best part of this brief respite was exploring the city and spending time with Liz and Emily. Seeing them had made me feel as if I had been gone for years, and, although I was excited to complete the remaining miles, it was wrenching to leave them. As I navigated my way out of Austin that morning, I knew that I would be listening to plenty of mournful cowboy ballads on my iPod for the next few days as I grappled with loneliness.

twelve

Austin to Leakey, Texas
Total Ride Mileage: 1,475

After the few days off in Austin, my body had clearly convinced itself that we were done with this absurd cross-country trip and voiced its displeasure through various aches and creaking sounds emanating from my joints as I pedaled. I put them out of mind as I approached the town of Henly, where the beauty of the Texas Hill Country began to reveal itself. Wildflowers, oak trees, and switch grass filled the scenery alongside pale-dirt ranch roads that disappeared into the mesquite miles away. Although it didn't do much for my muscles, spring in the Hill Country was something that certainly replenished the soul.

By the time I reached Johnson City 50 miles later, my tank was empty. I checked into a cheap motel, showered, and went for a walk downtown to stretch my legs before finding a place for dinner. This small community with a population of fewer than 1,200 people was once the hometown of President Lyndon Johnson. From my childhood, I remember seeing him on our black-and-white RCA TV almost every night as a powerful, booming, larger than life man. Now, as I walked past his small childhood home and the wooden porch from where he launched his senatorial and presidential campaigns, I was struck by how he was able to rise to such prominence from these humble beginnings.

A short distance from Johnson's house, I saw the headquarters of Pedernales Electric Cooperative. It was a reminder of one of President Johnson's most significant legislative successes. In his series *The Years of Lyndon Johnson*, author Robert Caro provides a moving account of what life was like in the Hill Country before electricity. It was a particular hardship for the women running the households, who had to rely on physical labor instead of appliances. Among his many accomplishments, Johnson considered bringing electricity to the Hill Country to be one of the most important.

The next morning after a restful sleep, I got an early start and left Johnson City before sunrise. I glided silently through the countryside for about 10 miles until I rode past a neglected wooden home that looked like it had been built in a past century. From its porch came the high-pitched wheezing yelp of an angry dog. "Not again," I thought. As I readied to accelerate, I quickly glanced over my shoulder at my pursuer, expecting to see a pit bull or other attack dog. Instead, moving unsteadily down the porch steps toward me was, perhaps, the most pathetic member of the canine family to have ever existed. This dog was an obese mongrel about the size and shape of a large watermelon. He was missing large swatches of fur along his sides and had one ear that appeared to have been chewed off. The poor guy also had only three legs. Deficiencies aside, he was committed to doing his job.

I figured I was in need of some good dog karma. Sizing up my opponent, I decided to let this old warrior have one last day in the sun and slowed to a pace that made it difficult to stay balanced. Gradually, the dog gained on me and eventually hopped to within striking distance of my foot. At that point, I feigned a mixture of surprise and fear and pedaled vigorously away, while he continued barking and asserting his primacy.

From Johnson City, I rode past Stonewall and, a few miles later, the Johnson Ranch, where LBJ and Lady Bird retired after his years in the Oval Office. Nearby, I saw two young men lugging overloaded backpacks on the opposite site of the road, one walking energetically in front of the other, who was shuffling a few yards behind. I pulled across the highway, introduced myself, and walked with them for a while. Matt and Scott were recent college graduates who were crossing the country on foot. Matt, who was walking in front, had started in New York. In locked outstretched arms, he held a long pole with a large American flag.

"Don't your arms getting tired carrying that?" I asked.

"They do, but this walk is important. People need to know what's going on."

"What do you mean?"

"Big Government is controlling every aspect of our lives. There's too much regulation. Too much taxation. And not enough accountability in Washington.

We've got to get rid of the government. I'm marching across the country on behalf of the Tea Party to help take back our country!"

Matt was serious and almost evangelistic in his view that the American way of life would be over unless citizens overthrew the grip of those in Washington D.C. I tried to engage him in a discussion about some of his political beliefs, pointing out that he was enjoying the benefits of a federal government that was providing a military force to protect the country, a Food and Drug Administration to insure that his food was safe, and even funding for the highway he was hiking along, but it was a frustrating attempt. Like many of his fellow countrymen, Matt appeared to view the First Amendment as an exclusive personal grant, providing only him the right to speak; he seemed to have no interest in listening to any views contrary to his own. He also seemed to be unaware of the obvious irony that he was marching on behalf of the Tea Party in front of the former home of the author of the Great Society.

Slightly exasperated, I fell back and walked with Scott for a few minutes.

"Did you start out with Matt in New York?" I asked.

"No, I had to finish school, so I met him in Louisiana after the semester ended and started there."

"How's it going?"

"This is my second pair of hiking boots. And I have huge blisters on every part of my feet. There have been some days over the last couple of months where I came close to quitting, my feet hurt so badly. Many times it's all I think of. Well, about that and a cold beer. I could really use a cold beer. Know where I can find one?"

Now, here, I thought, was a true American.

The next morning I celebrated "Laundry Day" in the town of Ingram. With only three changes of riding clothes, I found it was important to take advantage of whenever I found a "washateria," as the laundromats are called in this area. After many weeks on the road, I'd become somewhat immune to my own travelling aroma and had taken to wearing the same clothes for multiple days. Occasionally, when I stopped for lunch at the counter of a local diner, I would notice fellow patrons seated near me hurriedly finish their food and ask for the check. When this happened, it was a good indicator that it was time to grab a shower and do the laundry. Leaving Ingram, I traveled a few miles past the town of Hunt, where I visited one of the more unusual sights I'd seen in my travels. I had crossed over the Guadalupe River and climbed past some small ranches, and there it was, situated in a large open field: Stonehenge II.

On a whim in 1989, two local ranchers, Al Shepperd and Doug Hill, decided to create a replica of Stonehenge, the prehistoric monument discovered near Salisbury, England. Local lore has it that the project started when Hill gave Shepperd a large piece of limestone left over from one of his projects. Shepperd planted the stone upright in the middle of several acres of green pasture he owned in this area of the Texas Hill country. The vertical stone looked interesting, so what the heck? The men decided to add to it and make an arch. The arch looked even more impressive, and from there, things kind of got out of hand. When the available limestone ran out, the men started making monoliths that were steel and concrete, not stone as in the original Stonehenge, but they ended up creating a strikingly realistic representation.

As I wandered around taking pictures, the only person here on this warm spring day, two things came to mind. First, how strange it was to see this representation of iconic British and world history in a remote field in West Texas.

And, second, that Al and Doug clearly had too much time on their hands.

After reversing back over the Guadalupe River and traveling a few more miles, I passed "Boot Hill Ranch," which had a conspicuous way of identifying itself: extending more than a quarter-mile, every post in front of the ranch was topped by an old boot or shoe. There were hundreds of them in every size, color, and style imaginable—well-worn cowboy boots, old Red Wing work shoes, green rubber Wellingtons, even a pair of nylon après ski boots from the 1970s. Texas wasn't playing fair. How could one not appreciate a state where the citizens used their fence lines as shoetrees?

Entering the rolling hills of Kerr County, I had clear, windless, warm weather for a change and used the opportunity to strip down to my T-shirt and let the heat saturate my bones as I pedaled. I passed a series of small fenced ranches, one of which had a flagpole in the front yard. Underneath the Stars and Stripes, a camel causally noshed on some hay. In disbelief, I stopped to confirm what I was seeing. Yes, it was, indeed, a camel. Later, I passed another ranch with a mesh fence circling its perimeter and startled what appeared to be a herd of African impalas. Between Stonehenge II, Boot Hill Ranch, and this menagerie, I began to think that perhaps I was getting a bit too much sun. But I wasn't hallucinating. I would later learn that due to declining beef prices, some of the ranchers in the area had switched from breeding cattle to raising exotic animals for hunting and private zoos. I tried to call to mind an image of John Wayne telling his men to "saddle up" to drive a herd of ostriches, zebras, impalas or giraffes, but my decades of watching cowboy movies would not permit such blasphemy.

As I climbed higher into the Hill Country, the scenery became more alluring. Mats of prickly pear covered the landscape along with yellow Texas primrose and oaks just starting to leaf. The road was mine alone for hours at a time. As the sun started to swing west, I focused on the cadence of my pedals' shadows on the pavement to the accompaniment of Miles Davis on my headphones. The solitude, the subtle beauty of the surroundings, and the emotional pull of Miles' horn: It was bliss.

I hardly recognized myself anymore. It wasn't just the loss of a few pounds from my former "Dockers" physique or the addition of some scruffy facial hair. It was more than physical. With each turn of the crank, I felt the hardened shell that we develop as adults slowly dissolve and some internal battery begin to recharge. I was having difficulty recalling the work stresses that had inspired weeks of insomnia just a few months before. When I did, I smiled with the realization of how insignificant they were. I was finding perspective. I felt lighter. In both weight and spirit.

Late in the afternoon, I passed my intended campsite at Lost Maples State Natural Area, but decided to keep riding, unwilling to let the day end. At a small market in the hamlet of Vanderpool, I pulled over when I spotted a fully loaded touring bike parked out front. Inside, I met its owner, a man who looked to be in his mid-sixties, who was riding east. While he purchased his groceries, we discussed our routes, and he advised me against going any farther because it was getting dark and the hills between Vanderpool and Leakey were steep and dangerous—giving this area its nickname the "Alps of Texas." I thanked him for the advice but told him I still felt like riding. At that point, what had been a normal exchange between fellow cyclists grew heated, as he became surprisingly agitated and angry: "Fine! Don't listen to me!" Then he swept his groceries off the counter into a plastic bag, turned, and stormed out without another word.

Evidently, someone was suffering from an extreme case of chafing and didn't have his Desitin.

A few miles outside of Vanderpool, I hit the first climb. It was an 11% grade for two miles with only one slight bend. Nasty. This was followed a few miles later by a second climb of about three miles and a 9% grade and then a last short climb with a 10% grade. By comparison, the steep climbs in the Tour de France average between 7-12%. And those riders aren't carrying extra clothing, books, laptop, camera, and several 20-ounce cans of beer.

While the climbs were tough, the descents were equally daunting. In physics, terminal velocity is the speed at which driving forces are canceled out by resistive forces. I discovered that terminal velocity for my fully loaded bike was 35 mph. That was the fastest speed I could attain given air pressure and wind resistance. Or maybe it was just terminal velocity for my courage, because once I hit that speed, I was crushing the brake levers, feeling very much like I was trying to stop an out-of-control big rig.

Despite this distraction, the area grew even more beautiful with the setting sun. The angle of light brought texture, color, dimension, and grace to my surroundings. Each inhalation conveyed delicate desert fragrances into my nose and lungs. Finally, after a full day in motion, I slowed my bike to a stop at a motel in the small town of Leakey just as the first stars appeared overhead.

thirteen

Leakey to Seminole Canyon State Park, Texas
Total Ride Mileage: 1,619

I awoke the next morning groggy and disoriented—the result of the long, hard ride of the previous day. Lying under my blanket, slowly looking around the room, I took measure of my surroundings: a small, rustic, log cabin-style motel room with a late 1950s décor. My eyes alighted on a sign on the shelf opposite me: "Please do not use bathroom towels to clean bikes, motorcycles or guns."

Ah, that's right. I was in Texas.

Pulling my stiff body out of bed, I poured some hot water into a paper cup from the rusted bathroom tap and stirred in some instant coffee. Then, a few minutes later, I felt resourceful (or maybe just lazy) and stirred in a packet of instant oatmeal as well. I'm not sure why, but I just sensed it was going to be a tough day.

When I stepped out of my hotel room at 8:30 a.m., it was already pushing the mid-70s with high humidity and a cloudless, unrelenting sky. As I squinted my eyes in the harsh sunlight and looked at the empty road outside my motel, a single thought repeated in my brain: "You should quit."

On days like this, which thankfully were rare, I would go through a bit of mental gymnastics to persuade myself to keep riding. First, I would imagine the difficult logistics of abandoning my ride and flying home. I'd need to find how to get to the nearest major airport with my bicycle and gear—in some places this was several hundred miles distant. Leakey, for example, was so small it didn't have a car rental agency and I never saw a taxi or bus during my few hours there. So, I'd have to hitch a ride on a pickup or cattle truck. Assuming I solved this problem, I would have the challenge of finding a box large enough to pack everything. Then, I'd need to find a flight. The entire process could make it days before I was home. If that line of thinking didn't convince me to keep riding I'd resort to the big persuasion, which was to visualize explaining to friends and family that I had quit and ended my ride early without the excuse of an injury or major mechanical breakdown. The imaginary conversation with my children was usually what it took. I'd think about how differently they would view me when they knew I had given up. Then, I'd let out a deep sigh, take a drink from my water bottle, clip into my pedals and start moving for at least one more day.

After several hours and a series of grueling climbs in the exposed sun, I was feeling sore, empty, and just plain miserable. It was then that I spotted a large group of women heading east on bicycles. When one of them stopped to wait for a friend, I used it as an excuse to pull over and rest. We spoke for a few minutes as more than a dozen women sailed past. They were part of group of friends, all between 60 and 70 years old, who were riding across Texas with a van following behind with their food and gear. Starting that day from the town of Camp Wood, they had already covered more than three times my distance, including a very steep and prolonged climb. But each of the women seemed energetic and healthy—practically glowing. I'd seen that look before. When Liz and her girlfriends completed a long ride, they looked similarly euphoric.

I've always been fascinated with collective nouns, as in a "wake" of buzzards, an "ambush" of tigers, or a "passel" of possum. What, I thought, as I rested by the side of the road, would be the appropriate collective noun to describe a group of female riders? Finally, it hit me: a "perky," as in, "A perky of female cyclists just cycled past."

When you use it, please give me attribution.

A few hours later I reached Camp Wood and stopped for lunch. Camp Wood, a former lumber town of fewer than 900 citizens located near the Nueces River, is an example of how every community, regardless of size, has a story to tell. For Camp Wood it took place in 1924, when the town received an unexpected visit from a young aviator. The visit was unexpected because the aviator was off course and forced to land on Main Street. If that wasn't exciting enough for the local citizenry, the aviator cemented his place in town lore when, upon takeoff, he clipped a wing on a telephone pole and smashed into the local hardware store. His name? Charles Lindbergh.

The heat grew in intensity as I left Camp Wood and pedaled several hours toward Brackettville. My skin felt parched and thin, as if I were molting. When I saw a bridge that spanned the Nueces River, I took the opportunity to unsaddle and climb under the bridge to cool down and drain one of my water bottles in the shade. A large colony of chimney swifts was nesting nearby, and hundreds were in flight around me. Watching their effortless speed and agility made me feel even more sluggish by comparison.

Back on my bike, the ride continued as a hot, painful slog. The misery was compounded by a roadway with a tar and aggregate finish that increased the friction on my wheels and vibrated the frame as if I were riding endless miles of cobbles of the famous Paris-Roubaix bicycle race. It was a slow and stuttering ride under a scalding sun.

Twenty-five miles farther, the road separated from the river and the scenery became remarkable only for the constant heat shimmering off the asphalt. I kept pushing ahead, mile after mile, under the blazing sun, taking occasional breaks from the more than 90-degree temperature in the shade of cottonwood trees. I felt increasingly lightheaded and even slightly nauseated and the word "dehydration" flashed strobe-like in my mind as I began to ration the last sips of my water.

I was spent.

Finally, as I pedaled up a slight rise, I saw a man operating a construction grader who gave me a friendly wave from behind a cloud of dirt. He was the first person I had seen in more than five hours. A few minutes after passing him, I came upon a truck parked on the side of road. A tall Hispanic man hailed me from inside the cab. As I drew to a stop, he said: "Hot day for a ride. Would you like some cold water?" I looked at my empty bottles, nodded appreciatively, and gave thanks to the amazing generosity of strangers.

After a few long gulps of water, I began to revive. While I filled my plastic bottles from his large orange water jug, I asked what they were building.

"We're fencing a ranch," he said. "It's a pretty big job, a few hundred acres in all. We 'doze it flat, install the posts, and then the fencing. 'Round here most people use eight-foot steel mesh."

"Is that to contain cattle?" I asked.

"Nah, beef prices in this area have tanked in the last few years. Most of the ranchers now raise game to bring in more income. This ranch has white-tailed deer. The one down the road has exotic game."

"Ah! That explains it. I've seen what I've thought were African animals, like impalas on a couple of ranches."

"Yep, they're all around this area. Hunters don't have to travel to Africa to get the head on the wall. Now, they just come to Texas," he said with a grin.

"Let me ask you: As I've been travelling the last few days, I've seen these discarded bags on the side of the roadways labeled "deer corn." Does that have anything to do with this?"

"Oh, yeah. Lotta deer hunters 'round here. They pay the ranchers for each one they take down. To make sure that the hunters are successful, the ranchers load feed or "deer corn" into automatic feeders that are set to release the food at the same time each day. This trains the deer to regular feedin' times. The hunters sit above the feeders in elevated blinds throwin' back a few cold ones, wait for the deer to approach the feeders, and then… Blam!" he said, breaking into laughter.

Great, I thought. America's sedentary lifestyle had now debased even hunting. The next thing you know, the folks at La-Z-Boy are going to be selling recliners with rifle and shotgun mounts.

My thirst now quenched, I thanked the gentleman for his kindness and started riding again. An hour later, with the sun still high overhead, I finally reached Brackettville and checked into the small, spartan hotel at Fort Clark Springs. This former military base had an interesting history; for the latter half of the 19th century, the famed Buffalo Soldiers and the Seminole-Negro Indian Scouts were stationed here, both of which served with the U.S. Army in the fight against the Comanche. But my interest was not in the past, but in the pool—the Fort's large spring-fed swimming pool. I changed my clothes in my room and headed off for a dip, feeling anything but perky.

The ride into Del Rio the next morning was my fastest of the trip. I had a nice tailwind and, for a portion of the ride a road like a Brunswick pool table: smooth and flat. From the slightly elevated perch of my bicycle seat, I felt as if I could see the curvature of the earth over the horizon. A scissor-tailed flycatcher with its long trailing split tail flew in front of me followed by a number of summer tanagers. A few weeks before, bright red cardinals were in abundance. They were now replaced by the tanagers, indicating that I was moving into the West. Their flashing red wings were like avian semaphore signals against the tan and olive hues of the early morning desert.

For most of my life, I had paid little attention to birds. Like most people, I could identify no more than 10 species with names like "crow," "pigeon," and "seagull." Then, a decade ago, a friend and I hired a guide who led us on a kayak trip off Ellesmere Island in the far reaches of Northern Canada. As we were paddling one day, I noticed a medium-sized white bird with a black-topped head that seemed to hover above us; this seemed strange, since I thought that only hummingbirds possessed that ability. In response to my question, our guide spent the next few minutes telling us about the bird—an Arctic Tern—its habitat, reproduction, nesting habits, and amazing 12,000-mile annual migration. From that moment, I was hooked; to the extreme mortification of family and friends, I became a "birder." Sometimes, life is like that. One moment. One person. One conversation. And your life is forever enriched.

As I rode along Highway 90 in the foggy dawn, I saw headlights creeping toward me on an adjacent dirt road. As they approached, I noticed it was a border patrol officer driving slowly with his head out the window of his light green SUV. Watching him closely, I realized he was scanning the dirt, looking for footprints. It was a scene I would see repeated throughout the day as I saw more than a dozen officers walking or driving along the road searching for undocumented immigrants.

I arrived in Del Rio in time for an early breakfast. Like most border towns in the West, Del Rio was a bit run-down and chaotic, with a mélange of cultures expressed in the billboards, storefronts, and sounds. Signs were written alternately in English and Spanish. Radios of idling pick-ups blared either classic rock or ranchero music. Fast food restaurants advertised menudo or McNuggets. It was crowded and noisy, and I couldn't wait to get the hell out of the place.

The rest of the day sped by. With a 30-mph tailwind, my panniers became spinnakers pushing me down the road, past the surprisingly large Amistad

Reservoir (almost 850 miles of shoreline), and toward the town of Comstock. Twenty miles west of Del Rio, I found myself in line behind a row of trucks and cars that had slowed at an immigration checkpoint. It was an extensive operation with five border patrol officers, several sniffer dogs, and an array of video cameras focused on each vehicle. After they searched the truck ahead of me, I coasted to a stop and considered making a joke about carrying undocumented immigrants in my panniers. Instead, I looked at the serious faces and mirrored sunglasses surrounding me, thought better of it, gave them a smile and said: "Just me." They took a few moments to ask about my route and then waved me ahead.

Two hours later, I rolled into Seminole Canyon State Park and found a campsite located atop a small hill that provided an expansive view of endless miles of desert. The ranger station was closed when I arrived, so I found a site and set up my bivy sack and stove. I was enjoying my dinner on a picnic bench and absorbing the beauty of the desert at day's end when I felt something brush against my legs. I looked down and noticed my visitor—a large skunk. My initial reaction was to immediately go into full "Three Stooges" mode; you know, where they wave their hands over their faces and run in place in panic. Instead, mustering my courage, I restrained myself and sat still, perfectly still, until my guest took a sniff of my cycling shoes and found them even more foul than its own scent and scurried off.

After finishing dinner, I took a walk around the campground. Given that it was the off season, all the sites were vacant except for one where a small yellow tent was pitched next to a fully outfitted BMW motorcycle with front and rear black saddlebags. Seated on a nearby bench was a tall, attractive young woman with curly black hair. Lorraine introduced herself with a warm handshake and asked me to join her for a cup of tea. (Cue Middle-Aged Male Fantasy No. 2,829.) She had arrived alone in San Francisco a few weeks earlier and purchased her motorcycle with the intent of circumnavigating the U.S. before returning home to England. In her charming voice (British accent? I'm in love.), she told of her travels through California and the Southwest. She explained that she was between jobs as a massage therapist (Thank you, sweet Jesus!), making the timing for such a trip perfect. Plus, she needed some time alone because she was just getting over a bad breakup with her girlfriend (Wait…What? Girlfriend?).

After a few minutes sharing stories of our travels, and with my middle-aged male fantasies vanquished, we sat quietly together enjoying our tea and watching the sky change from vermillion to scarlet to blush, and listening to the black-throated sparrows in the surrounding cacti. Their calls provided a soothing soundtrack as we watched the sun setting at the desert's end.

fourteen

Seminole Canyon State Park to Sanderson, Texas
Total Ride Mileage: 1,700

The barrenness of this part of the Texas desert country was haunting. Other than a few modern structures in the park—a roadway, telephone lines, a small visitor center—there was only a seemingly endless expanse of cacti, creosote brush, and rust-colored soil. Yet more than 4,000 years ago this area was inhabited by a semi-nomadic group known as the Pecos People. I learned this the next morning when I toured the intricate cliff paintings they had left in the park to delight future generations of touring cyclists.

Not much is known about the Pecos People; no current Native Americans count them in their lineage. However, anthropologists do know what they ate. While excavating the site, a large volume of coprolite was discovered. Coprolite is, to put it delicately, fossilized fecal matter. (I once brought my son a piece of coprolite—dinosaur dung—from a trip to Utah thinking that it would be interesting, if not funny, to a ten-year-old. Given his disappointed reaction, I should have opted for a T-shirt instead.) Using the coprolite, scientists were able to reconstitute the original matter and determined that the Pecos People lived on fish, deer, lizards, grass, twigs, cactus, and insects—in other words, a true subsistence diet. Looking at the desolate and desiccated countryside surrounding me, I was astounded to think that anyone could survive here.

Rejoining Highway 90 and heading west, I passed another border patrol truck, this one using chains to drag three large tires over the same dirt frontage road that I had seen the previous day, raking it clean to make it easier to see footprints. A few miles farther, across that same dirt road, lay a series of thin pieces of particle board placed like stepping stones, perhaps left by undocumented immigrants surprised in the act of crossing the previous evening and unable to retrieve the boards. I never found out for certain, but it was a scene that illustrated the challenges of the nation's immigration policy.

Ten miles east of Langtry, I stopped to rest on a bridge spanning the legendary Pecos River. Broad, turbulent and muddy, the river was far more impressive than I had imagined from my many years of watching cowboy movies. The countryside for the previous few days had conveyed that same western cinematic feel. However, it wasn't because of the scenery, but the sounds. In those classic John Ford movies, the wind blows continuously; it is a character revealed through squeaky saloon doors, rattling chains, and spinning weather vanes. I heard these same noises as I pedaled the roads in this expanse of Texas—windmill blades creaked, road signs vibrated, corrugated tin roofs rattled, fence gates swung open and slammed shut, and tumbleweeds the size of tires scratched across the roadway. Given the setting, I kept expecting Gus, Call, and the rest of the Hat Creek gang from *Lonesome Dove* to emerge on horses from the sagebrush at any moment.

The town of Langtry was a faint spot on the map with a population of fewer than 50. More than a century ago, it was famed as the location where the legendary Judge Roy Bean held court in his saloon billing himself as the "Law West of the Pecos." Between court hearings, Bean adjourned to his bar, served drinks and entertained with stories of his love for the British actress Lillie Langtry, allegedly the source of the town's name.

In order to increase tourism, the state had funded a small visitor center and museum in Langtry. I used its air conditioning as an additional enticement to learn more about the Hon. Judge Bean and spent an hour exploring the remains of Bean's courthouse, saloon and some of his personal possessions. In one section of the museum, I came across a portion of one of Bean's judicial decisions. After finding $41 in cash and a handgun on someone who had been shot to death, Bean ruled:

> "It is the duty of the court to confiscate this concealed weapon, which is a dam' good gun because it is legally ag'inst the law, especially (for) a dead man. And in view of the evidence I find it the court's duty to fine the offender forty-one simoleons for carryin' concealed weapons."

I have studied many judicial decisions during my career as an attorney. Rarely have I come across one that was as humorous to read. Were he alive today, Judge Bean would have been a natural for television's *"The People's Court"*.

Other than the museum, the town bore little resemblance to its storied past—just a few small ranch-style homes surrounded by the collapsing remains of wooden buildings with rusted tin roofs and broken windows, inhabited now only by tumbleweeds. To keep busy until evening, I kicked around the dirt streets and then walked down to the Rio Grande River that borders the southern edge of the town. Besides his occupations as saloon keeper and judge, Bean was also a fight promoter, the Don King of his generation. In 1896, he decided to bring attention to Langtry by hosting a world-championship boxing match. One small problem interfered: Boxing matches at that time were illegal in both Texas and Mexico. That didn't deter the judge. He located a small island in the middle of the Rio Grande just beyond the town and state borders and used it as the site for the boxing ring while the fans sat along the riverbanks. Both the caliber of the fighters—heavyweights Bob Fitzsimmons of Australia and Peter Mahar of Ireland—and Judge Bean's marketing efforts brought attention to the town and thousands of visitors from around the world to the fight. As I walked above the riverbank, I found a post with a small plaque on an empty dirt hillside above the river; it is all that commemorates the event today.

There was no lodging or campgrounds in Langtry, but I had heard from someone at the museum that it was permissible to camp behind the town's small cinder block community center. No shower, no bathroom, no picnic table. Just a patch of dirt next to a rusty swing set that squeaked in the warm desert breeze. I rolled out my sleeping bag and bivy sack and enjoyed a cup of tea under the early evening light, imaging that I was a 21st-century member of the Hat Creek gang. Then I fell quickly asleep.

The rooster in the yard next door and a wild turkey hidden in the cactus behind the community center were awake before sunrise. Both were calling out in full volume, making it impossible to sleep. I was clearly an innocent bystander caught in the middle of an avian turf war. Rather than trying to broker a peace between these warring feathered factions, I shoved my sleeping bag and gear into my panniers and, with the first rays of dawn, headed down the road.

The ride toward Sanderson was long, hot, and monotonous, but at least there was no wind for a change. There was also little traffic on this stretch of the highway, and most vehicles were associated with the border patrol. By mid-morning, the day was warming, so I stopped in Dryden for a cold soft drink at the town's general (and only) store. Dryden had a population of approximately ten, and I met almost a third of the town while enjoying my beverage on a dilapidated couch in front of the store. Judging by the many buildings around me, most of them abandoned or boarded, Dryden must have once been a town of substance and vitality. Now, like many of the towns I had visited, little remained.

Since the 2008 fiscal meltdown, it's common to hear government leaders speaking about "Wall Street vs. Main Street." In much of America, however, Main Street no longer exists. It's become a romantic archetype of the past. I began my trip with a Rockwellian (as in Norman) vision of the places I would visit, including quaint town squares surrounded by local restaurants, taverns, markets, and hotels. While the squares still existed, in most towns the businesses were shuttered and replaced by fast food restaurants, chain hotels, and Walmart stores "out by the highway," as the locals would say. At times, it felt rather bleak and far removed from the halcyon days of our politicians' rhetoric.

I arrived exhausted and hungry in Sanderson late in the afternoon and ate an enormous dinner (salad, garlic bread, baked chicken, and two desserts—a piece of chocolate cake and a slice of apple pie) at a surprisingly good restaurant called the Roundhouse Café.

"You really were hungry!" exclaimed my waitress while clearing my many plates.

"Yes, and the food was wonderful, thank you."

"Where are you riding from?" she asked.

"I started in Florida, and I'm heading to my home in California, near San Francisco."

"That's a long piece. How did you train for this?"

"I didn't really. The extent of my training was Florida, Mississippi, and Alabama. I figured that because those states are flat, it would give me the chance to lose some weight before I hit the Rockies," I answered with a smile. As I said this, I noticed her eyes wandering over the caloric carnage of my meal and sensed that she doubted my strategy would be successful.

After dinner, I walked across the street and checked into the Outback Oasis Motel, unpacked, showered, and then stepped outside to watch the sunset. It had become a highlight of each day for me, a moment of contemplative communion with nature. When I did, the hotel's owners, Ruth and Roy, invited me over to a picnic table to enjoy a beer with them and another couple who were visiting from San Antonio. As we sat sipping our longnecks and looking out over the desert, Ruth shared that she and Roy were from Kansas where they had owned a pet shop for a number of years. Roy fell in love with the Sanderson area while hunting, and the couple decided to buy the motel and relocate five years earlier. Despite his new role as a hotelier, Roy could not let go of his passion for animals, especially reptiles. He now collected snakes and lizards from all over the Southwest and housed them in an empty wing of the motel. He kept offering to show them to me, but I declined and instead chose to enjoy the company, conversation, cold beer, and the warm Texas evening. (OK, I admit it. Belligerent dogs I can handle. Solicitous skunks—no problem. But snakes? They scare the crap out of me.)

fifteen

Sanderson to Davis Mountains State Park, Texas
Total Ride Mileage: 1,822

I started out before daybreak the next morning in the hope that I would be able to push the 85 miles to Alpine before the afternoon wind picked up. Ahead of me was darkness, fog, and a quiet, empty highway. But I wasn't alone. Large numbers of white-tailed deer were feeding along the roadside. Given the silence of my bicycle, they were frequently startled as I approached. Through the mist the flash of their tails looked like white exclamation marks registering surprise as they ran to find an opening in the fences to escape as I rode by.

As the clouds began to lift, I travelled through an area inhabited by seemingly hundreds of turkey vultures. I've never seen so many in one location. On one fence line alone there were dozens; each perched on a post, warming itself in the first rays of sunshine. They barely noticed my presence so I tried a bit of avian humor to draw their attention and as I pedaled by I dropped a tune on them from the classic rock band Kansas and sang loudly: "'Carrion' my wayward son…" Their apathy suggested that they also thought it was a lame bit of humor. To redeem myself, I offer you a Vulture Fun Fact. Unlike most mammals, birds have no sweat glands and are unable to cool themselves through perspiration. This presents a special problem for vultures because their large size and black coloring cause them to absorb significant heat during the day. To manage this, they have developed a special method to cool themselves. It's called "urohydrosis." In effect, the birds defecate and urinate on their scaly legs, and, as the excrement evaporates, it lowers their body temperature.

Personally, I prefer the air conditioner of a run-down motel room any day.

As I continued through the hazy early light, I spotted a small car parked next to a roadside rest stop with two high-performance racing bikes mounted on the roof. I slowed when the owner, leaning against the car and holding a mug of coffee, yelled out to me with a big grin:

"Traffic's horrible this morning isn't it?"

"Just dreadful. I hate the Sanderson rush hour," I replied, knowing instantly that I had met a kindred spirit.

Rich was a middle school biology teacher from Kansas and, on the weekends, an amateur bicycle racer. He was driving to Fort Davis to compete in a road race that weekend and had spent the night at this roadside stop sleeping in his car. For 20 minutes, we had a conversation that was a blur of bicycles, camping gear, traveling, and…snakes.

"They're all around here. In fact, this area between Sanderson and Fort Davis is one of the prime spots for herpetology study in the U.S. I come down here all the time to collect specimens," he said matter-of-factly.

"What kinds of snakes are there?" I asked with a wavering voice, knowing that I would not like the answer.

"Well, there are non-venomous ones like the king snake and garter snake. You also can find night and hognose snakes. But the ones I like to get are the rattlesnakes. There are about four or five types out here: black-tailed, prairie, Mojave and, of course, the western diamondback. They're all over the place at night."

"What?" I exclaimed. "You go tromping around here at night looking for poisonous snakes?"

"Sure. It's the best time to find them because they're active. I bagged a four-foot western last year."

In stunned silence, I made a mental pledge that I would not spend another night camping until I left Texas.

While I wanted to spend more time with Rich, I needed to get riding to avoid the afternoon wind. We shook hands, said our goodbyes, and agreed to try to connect 120 miles down the road near Fort Davis later in the week.

With the exception of a brief stop in the town of Marathon for lunch, I spent the rest of the day doing nothing but pedaling in the oppressive heat. Although the West Texas landscape was unvaried, it always offered something unexpected. In the empty desert a few miles before reaching Alpine, for example, I saw a large flat expanse in the dry sage lined with rows of identical white tombstones. A nearby sign identified it as "Arlington Southwest," an unoccupied cemetery with each tombstone representing a soldier from Texas killed in the war in Iraq. It was established and maintained by Veterans for Peace, a group of military veterans seeking alternatives to war. Again, not something I expected from the Lone Star State.

By late afternoon, when I finally reached Alpine, the temperature had reached the low nineties and I had consumed six bottles of water, including one that I dumped on my head to cool myself. (Thankfully, I had not had to resort to urohydrosis.) It had been a tough day's ride, and I decided to give myself a treat that evening and checked into an attractive place in downtown Alpine called the Holland Hotel. (Honestly, the choice to stay in a hotel instead of camp had nothing to do with Rich's snake stories.) The Holland was the type of hotel that was a fixture of many communities during the era in American history when the railroad was king. Situated across from the tracks and depot, it had been recently renovated with amenities that I had found in few of the motels I had stayed in over the previous weeks—little things, like toilet paper, unstained towels, and a shower without mold.

After I cleaned and changed, I walked to a nearby bar and met up with Don. Since separating before Austin, we had exchanged messages with updates on our progress and had agreed to rendezvous in town that evening. After a few beers in the crowded biker bar, we walked to a little Italian restaurant for dinner. Over pasta, I told Don of my time in Austin and adventures in Vanderpool, Del Rio, and Langtry. Of course, Don, who had taken a different route over the past week, then had to regale me with his stories of staying for a few days on a working cattle ranch and the experience of blowing out both of his tires in the space of a few minutes during a single day's ride. When this occurred, he was near Amistad Reservoir, miles from any bicycle store. Good fortune, however, smiled on Don with an excess of pearly white enamel.

"Yeah," he began, "you know that long, empty stretch along Amistad? Well, I'm riding along and 'Pow!' my back tire blows. And not just my tube, the whole side of my tire! I pull over to the side, unbolt the trailer, take off the wheel, and then change the tube and use a patch on the hole. Then I pull the rig back together and start riding again. I get about 100 yards when 'Pow!' the other tire blows. I pull over again but realize I have no more tubes, tires or patches."

"How could both tires fail? What did you ride over?" I asked.

"I think the tires blew because they were both worn, but I'm not sure why it happened in the same place. It wasn't glass or thorns or anything I could see. So I'm standing there trying to figure out what to do and thinking that the closest bike shop is 40 miles back in Del Rio. Then, out of nowhere, a pickup truck pulls over. The driver asks me if I'm OK. I explain what happened, and as I'm talking he notices my U.S. Marine Corps sticker on the back of the trailer."

(When I first met Don he mentioned that he had served in the Marines. Perhaps because he didn't look the part with his gray ponytail, he had decided to affix a Marine decal on the back of his trailer. He even offered one to me "just in case.")

Don continued: "So the guy asks: 'Were you in the Marines?' And, before I could say, 'Semper fi,' he helped me load my bike and trailer into the bed of his truck. Then he turned around and drove me back to Del Rio where I bought a new set of tires and tubes. Next, get this, the guy drives me all the way back to his house where he insists that I enjoy a home-cooked meal and meet his wife. Hell of a meal, too," he uttered with a look of extreme contentment.

Don was making this ride look far too easy.

For a change, I had a wonderful evening's respite. I've always been a bit of an insomniac, the result of too much coffee and work stress. Despite the physical exertion of the ride, I was still having difficulty sleeping because of my ever-changing surroundings. Each day, everything was different. I had traded a life of daily convention—shower, breakfast, commute, work, commute, dinner, sleep—to one in which all routine was absent.

Another reason was more prosaic. Having left my razor at home, my early rumblings of a beard constantly itched and kept me awake at night. A few weeks earlier I'd reconsidered the beard and purchased a razor, each day shaving any portion of my beard that was scratchy. The result was that I was now sporting what could only be described as a "Mennonite elder" chin beard. It looked incredibly silly, but solitary travel allows you to explore not only who you are, but even how you look.

After struggling to wake myself and get dressed, I strolled down the street and into the Bread & Breakfast Bakery Café. A sign out front said: "Hippies use the back door – no exceptions." Given my preconceived views of Texas, I wasn't sure if it was a meant to be humorous.

For the past weeks, my breakfast had been comprised of coffee and instant oatmeal or, perhaps, a doughnut crushed in my overflowing panniers. On some mornings, I just awoke and rode for hours until I found a fast food restaurant to fuel up. I know many cycling purists who take a disciplined approach to what they eat on a ride. They focus on consuming things like power bars, electrolyte drinks, and high-energy supplements in the form of various gels and tablets all in the name of achieving peak riding performance.

I am not one of those people.

Now I had the chance to have a real breakfast, and I took full advantage, stuffing my face with an omelet, sausage, and a giant warm cinnamon bun lathered in butter. As I ate, I listened to three older men at the next table wearing well-worn cowboy hats and western attire. They were engaged in a curmudgeonly debate of the merits of the recently passed federal health care bill. One of them, with a satirical grin, told his tablemates that the legislation was a disaster because young people would now have better access to health care, leading to "more of them" and "what the world really needs are more old farts like us." The three of them then discussed Texas politics and ended up swapping favorite quotes of famed Texan liberal satirist, Molly Ivins. Somehow, it wasn't quite what I expected. Once again, Texas was challenging my stereotypes.

After breakfast, I walked a few blocks down the street past the movie theatre (children $3, adults $5) and a giant mural that included the visage of Dan Blocker, who went to college here. For those of a certain age, you will recall him as "Hoss" from the TV show *Bonanza*. A few blocks further, I found Front Street Books, a wonderful independent bookstore. It was located in two buildings on either side of a street, but only one of them was staffed. You walked into the other, selected your item, and then took it across the street to be purchased. No surveillance cameras, no electronic anti-theft tags, no clerks hovering over you—just trust. Welcome to small-town America.

For days, I had been subjected to intense skies during cloudless days. Mornings and evenings provided unparalleled beauty, but, for the hours in between, the sun overhead was unrelenting. The heat transformed my helmet into a steam cooker, and sweat would stream down my face as I pedaled, mixing with the sunscreen I constantly applied. Perhaps it was my growing confidence that a tangle between my bicycle and a car was unlikely on the open roads of the area, but I decided to relegate my helmet to the rack on the back of my bike and to try a different approach. In a local drugstore, I purchased an Alpine Cowboys baseball cap (the local minor league team) with its "06" logo reflecting the team's owner since 1946, the local Kokernot 06 Ranch. It didn't provide as much protection as a helmet, but it made for far more comfortable riding and even elicited an occasional wave from local fans of the team.

The miles into the town of Fort Davis were flat and uneventful, but still scenic. On either side of the road stretched plains of dried grass and century plants—to the west, a backdrop of giant knuckles of rust-colored mesas. Ft. Davis, although much smaller than Alpine, was equally inviting, containing a number of shops and historical museums and landmarks. It even had a small gourmet grocery store named Stone Village Market. After weeks of searching to find even a fresh apple or banana, it was as if I had stumbled upon a culinary oasis. The aisles were filled with a variety of organic fruits and vegetables, gourmet coffees, a full deli, even a bakery. It gave me a glimmer of what it must be like for an immigrant from an impoverished country visiting our "Land of Plenty." I was overwhelmed by the diversity of choices as I stocked up on food for dinner and snacks for the next few days, including an assortment of cheese, some fresh baked bread, pasta, apples and cookies until my panniers were overloaded.

On the way to my campground for the evening, I detoured to visit the historical park containing portions of the fort for which the town was named and founded. Fort Davis was a key outpost from the 1850s to 1890s protecting white settlers in the area between El Paso and San Antonio against the Mescalero Apaches. The historical park contained both the remains of the original fort and a reconstructed barracks and parade ground. But what I found most interesting was located adjacent to the park; I was getting ready to leave, when I noticed a small pioneer graveyard overgrown with weeds and dotted with dozens of faded stone markers, some dating back more than 150 years. Judging by its condition, it was a memorial rarely visited by tourists.

Next to one unkempt gravesite, a faded metal plaque told the story of a woman whose fiancée had been kidnapped by Apaches on their wedding night.

As the weeks passed with no sign of her husband, the woman, through worry and loneliness, gradually became deranged. She would spend every evening, until her death 30 years after the kidnapping, climbing to the top of the nearby mountains to light a signal fire in the hope that her fiancée would use it to find his way home. He never did. As I left the cemetery, I thought about the constant flow of messages from Liz and our children. Whether it was a text from Declan at college, an email from Emily or Bryce or a phone call with Liz, my family was constantly with me. They had become my signal fire as I headed home.

After leaving the fort, I walked across the street to a shop that advertised birding supplies, gourmet wine, antiques, fudge, and a small museum in honor of a former major league baseball player, Wally Moon. (As a fan of our national pastime, I am embarrassed to say that I didn't recall Mr. Moon. I should have, not because he had a very successful 12-season career with teams such as the Cardinals and Dodgers, but because he possessed possibly the greatest unibrow in baseball history. Track down one of his baseball cards and see if you don't agree.)

A curious thing about small towns in America is that, with the exception of gas stations, markets, and real estate offices, local businesses can't afford to specialize; there just isn't a large enough customer base. As a result, they must offer a greater variety of goods to be successful, which is why you find a video store that also serves pizza, a garden shop with a tanning booth and nail salon, and a birding-wine-antiques-fudge store that has a museum dedicated to a former major league baseball player.

Four miles down the road I arrived at Davis Mountains State Park and met Don at the campsite he had reserved for us for the night. It was a large space situated under the shade of a group of cottonwood trees bordered by a creek bed that contained the last traces of winter rains. Don set up his tent near the trees, and I rolled out my sleeping bag in an open area near the creek that looked perfect for stargazing. With all of the savory food from the market, we decided to celebrate with a feast complete with a nice bottle of pinot noir.

Now, for your pleasure, a survivor skills test. You are camping on the edge of the Chihuahuan Desert. The temperature is approaching 90 degrees. You have no ice. How do you keep your pinot at an appropriate temperature for optimal consumption?

(a) You ask a neighboring camper to keep it in his cooler and trust that he won't drink it or leave before you retrieve it.

(b) This is a trick question. Touring cyclists only drink beer or grain alcohol—never something as effete as wine.

(c) You store it in the toilet tank in the campground bathroom.

If you chose (c), you would be correct. Don was a genius.

Our repast that evening was a wonderful collection of cheeses, crackers, fresh fruit, and, of course, cleverly chilled wine. As Don and I were preparing our meal, Rich, the cyclist I had met outside Sanderson, stopped by our campsite to say hello. He could only stay briefly, since he was on his way for some nocturnal snake wrangling. I was thankful that he didn't invite us to join because I'm certain Don would have agreed and dragged me along.

A few minutes after Rich left, Larry, a cyclist staying in a nearby campsite, walked over and introduced himself, and we invited him to join us for dinner. Larry was riding eastbound across the country from Seattle. He had been laid off from his job as a city planner a few months earlier. For him the ride was an opportunity to figure out what was next and to explore the forgotten urban landscapes of the communities along his route. As we ate, he shared with us his architectural insights and ideas about how to use downtown restoration projects to revitalize the declining towns we had seen as we pedaled the country. Fueled by camaraderie and pinot, the three of us talked for hours without pause, enjoying a wonderful Texas evening beneath a sky filled with so many stars, it was difficult to identify constellations.

sixteen

Davis Mountains State Park to Fort Hancock, Texas
Total Ride Mileage: 1,977

The following day was pure, endless drudgery. Don had decided to spend another day lounging at the campsite, while I chose to get moving. Another mistake. It was an 85-mile, 10-hour slog to Van Horn into a wind gusting with such velocity that the phone lines screeched like the voices of wraiths.

To make the day even more of a challenge, the previous evening had afforded me little sleep. After climbing into my sleeping bag, I noticed a skunk wandering nearby. Whenever it came within arm's reach, I would try to coax it away, only to receive a raised tail warning in response. Then the javelinas arrived. I had read stories about how these mid-sized peccaries could do real damage with their tusks when provoked. In my wine-induced haze, I questioned whether I might be provoking them simply by lying quietly in my sleeping bag; I finally concluded that they would eventually move away.

At first they stuck to the brush surrounding the campsite, but gradually they moved closer, becoming more intrusive and aggressive. I tried to ignore them and buried my head deep in my bag, but their nearing, croup-like snorts and grunts made sleep impossible. Out of frustration (and a bit of fear), I left the ground to the skunks and javelinas and grabbed a perch atop the picnic table. This proved workable until I fell asleep and rolled off the tabletop, striking the bench seat with a loud "thwack." Stunned, disoriented, and with an aching head, I finally surrendered and sat cross-legged atop the table with my sleeping bag draped over me as I watched under the bright starlight as dozens of javelinas moved slowly through the campsite like a flotilla of small destroyers. It wasn't until after 3 a.m. that they finally disappeared, and I was able to move back to the ground and catch at least a few hours of sleep.

A few days later, when I next reconnected with him, Don recounted a conversation he had with a park ranger who had stopped by the campsite after I had departed. Don mentioned to him all the javelinas I had reported from the previous night. In response, the ranger pointed to a well-worn path to the creek (that I had clearly overlooked) and explained that my sleeping bag had been placed in the middle of the thoroughfare the javelinas used each night to access the last remaining water in the creek.

While fighting the wind up a deserted stretch of highway toward Van Horn, I spied a solitary building in the distance. Except for this structure, the road, and the power lines, there was no evidence of humans anywhere on the horizon. Hoping it might be a small store with food and cold drinks, I grew excited and increased my speed. As I drew nearer, it turned out not to be a market, but…a Prada store? I dismounted from my bicycle and walked around the building in confusion. It was closed, but through the windows I saw shelves and displays of various Prada luxury products, including stylish handbags and high heel shoes that one would see in a shop in New York or Tokyo. Was I dehydrated? Hallucinating? Wandering about 25 feet from the building, I noticed a small sign hidden by a group of tumbleweeds that provided an answer. This store was the work of an artist from Marfa, a town to the south.

I may have been disappointed to miss out on a cold beverage, and I'll admit that I don't have a strong interest in contemporary art; however, I was struck by how surreal the installation was. It was made even more so by another nota-tion on the sign: "The family of the late Willer Alton 'Slim' Brown, (Trucker, Rancher, Roper, Friend) has generously contributed to the project by lending their land." One can only imagine how Slim's family reacted when the artist first described his project.

Late in the afternoon, I finally sighted Van Horn in the distance. Despite a long descent into town, the strong headwinds prevented me from coasting, and it was another hour before I pulled into a motel. It's a struggle to find a highlight to a visit to Van Horn, which is best described as a truck stop with a population of 2,200 people. The town's only real prominence came when John Madden, a former NFL coach and television announcer, once visited the local Chuy's Restaurant and named it to his "All Madden Hall of Fame" on a broadcast in the early 1990s. This event may represent the apex of Van Horn's history. Even if the town offered more of interest, I was too tired to see it. After downing a greasy burger, I flopped onto the bed completely exhausted. My legs were so stressed from the day's ride that they were vibrating like a tuning fork as I drifted to sleep.

It was after leaving Van Horn the following day, and having almost crossed the entire state of Texas, that I finally saw one. So much of Texas's cultural identity is tied to the longhorn breed of cattle that I had expected to see herds of them blanketing the landscape. But it was only here, within acres of fenced Chihuahuan Desert that I saw a solitary, massive bull. Its horns must have been six feet from tip to tip; strangely, one of them dipped downward at an abrupt angle like an ungulate dowsing rod.

Texas's association with the longhorn goes back to before the state was founded. For an early settler trying to scratch out an existence two centuries ago, cattle were often the difference between survival and the loss of a homestead. Settlers quickly discovered that the longhorn, although lean, was particularly well-equipped to survive the area's poor vegetation and was highly resistant to disease. As a result, the population of the longhorn grew until it covered the state and became the source of legendary cattle drives to the stockyards of Kansas City.

In the late 1800s, however, as ranges were replaced by fenced ranches and cattle drives by railroad cars (an inefficient transportation system for cattle with horns measuring seven to eight feet long), the longhorn population declined as ranchers turned to fatter breeds of cattle. By the early 1920s, the longhorn was almost extinct. In an attempt to preserve this part of Texas heritage, the U.S. Forest Service relocated a small herd of breeding stock to a refuge in Oklahoma. That herd became the source of much of today's remaining longhorn stock, including, in all likelihood, the bull standing before me. As I stood there looking at him I reflected on the ranches filled with African game, the unique fence line of Boot Hill Ranch, towns like Alpine and Austin, Stonehenge II, a Prada shop in the desert and the demise of the longhorn and I realized that every-thing I thought I knew about Texas was just plain wrong.

Sierra Blanca, the small town that I reached later in the day, bears witness to the American attitude that no one much cares if you come in second. A transcontinental railroad was joined with a silver spike here in 1881 when two competing railroads (the Southern Pacific and Missouri Pacific) agreed to link. Although it was a major accomplishment in its own right, this event occurred 13 years after the golden spike was hammered in the tracks of the first transcontinental railroad near Provo, Utah, in 1868. Here's what Sierra Blanca, as the second place winner, later won instead: worldwide recognition as home to one of the nation's largest sewage dumps, courtesy of New York City.

After Congress in the late 1980s banned dumping sewage into the ocean, the Big Apple had to find another location for disposing its waste. Eventually, Sierra Blanca was selected as a site. Over a six-year period, New York transported more than 200 tons of sludge each week to this remote burg of fewer than 500 people. Thank you, Big Apple!

This town, like many others I'd passed through in the previous weeks, was clearly in decline. Most of the businesses were shuttered or abandoned; only a handful were still in operation. One of them was a local eatery called Curly's Barbecue. Parking my bicycle outside, I entered to a décor that could best be described as 1970s yard sale. The interior was dark and dusty and adorned with old license plates, framed law enforcement patches, (two) plastic Frankenstein heads, stuffed animals, wind chimes, and other assorted items. Reverently displayed on one wall like a religious artifact was a neatly framed, autographed photo of country singer Reba McEntire.

I took a menu off the counter and pulled up a chair at a long communal table next to five men who had stopped in on their lunch break. One was a uniformed border patrol officer, and the others were local mechanics wearing greasy blue jumpsuits. They must have seen me arrive with my bicycle because they immediately started asking about my ride, appending each question with "Sir." As in:

"Sir, do you like Texas?"

"What has been the most challenging part of your ride, sir?"

"Have you had any trouble, sir?"

I assumed this deferential address was on account of my graying hair and Mennonite elder chin beard. Or it could have been that polite respect was just a way of life in this part of the world.

After answering their flurry of questions, I turned my attention to Rick, the border patrol officer. I described the border patrol activities I had seen over the past two weeks and inquired about his job and border patrol operations in that area. According to Rick, the border patrol had assigned more than 200 officers to the region around this small town to detect undocumented immigration and fight the drug trade. The violent drug cartels in Juarez (directly across the border from El Paso) were causing fearful Mexican citizens to flee for the safety of the United States. As a result, Rick and the rest of the border patrol were kept very busy.

I asked my tablemates what was good to eat, and, at the strong recommendation of one of the mechanics, I tried the "Curly's Special," consisting of five roasted poblano chiles smothered with shredded brisket and melted cheese—a heart attack on a plate. It tasted far better than I had expected, and the ensuing heartburn warmed me during the remainder of the day's ride.

seventeen

Fort Hancock, Texas, to Caballo Lake State Park, New Mexico
Total Ride Mileage: 2,146

During my career in the corporate world, I learned to actively manage my calendar. Each day there were meetings with employees, executives, and board members; conference calls with customers and outside counsel; and a myriad of other demands on my focus and attention. I found that unless the day was planned in detail, the needs of others would quickly overwhelm my ability to do my job effectively. It was a discipline that had become habit. But this discipline had to be abandoned on my ride. I struggled to be flexible and to plan just one thing each day: putting my butt on the leather saddle and heading west. Today was a good example. When I awoke, I thought it would be a relatively unremarkable day, with uninteresting scenery, ending in the city of El Paso. I was once again wrong.

As I left the Fort Hancock Motel and headed across the street to a cinder-block restaurant called Angie's for breakfast (the only restaurant I saw in town), I noticed something different: a tailwind! I've never been one to follow weather forecasts. Where I live in California, the weather is relatively consistent and rarely impacts life. The only challenge for local television weather forecasters in my hometown is to come up with novel ways to express "74 degrees and sunny." However, on this ride, I'd become a weather junkie, staring at clouds, checking the wind direction, seeking advice from locals, and reading any newspaper weather report with the intensity of a bookie studying *The Daily Racing Form*. The previous day's weather forecast had predicted a shift in winds to the west, and the breeze that morning confirmed that the forecast was correct.

After breakfast, I returned to my room, quickly packed my panniers, and walked my bicycle to the front desk to check out. In many of the small lodgings in the South like this one, the family that operated the motel was from India. Frequently, I would open the door to the lobby and be overwhelmed with the aroma of curry, tikka masala, and other mouthwatering dishes cooking in living quarters hidden nearby. Lobbies were often decorated with postcards or calendars from Punjab or Goa and with small figurines of Hindu deities.

More than half of all small motels in the United States are now operated by immigrants from India according to a recent study by a sociology professor from Oberlin College. Many of these motel managers belong to the more than 11,000 members of the Asian Hotel Operators Association. Most are small businessmen who reside with their families in the motels and rely on them as labor to operate the business.

This motel was an example. As I entered the lobby a middle-aged man in a short-sleeved polyester shirt, whom I assumed was the patriarch of the family, stood behind the cash register; behind him were what appeared to be his wife and mother, both resplendent in silk saris of turquoise and amber. As I paid my bill, I tried to strike up a conversation.

"Good morning, I'd like to check out of Room 17."

"Very good, sir." He said as he tabulated my bill on a handheld calculator.

"It looks like you and your family are from India. I've visited both Bangalore and Delhi."

He glanced furtively as his wife. "That will be $47.97, please."

"Unfortunately, I was there only on business," I continued, handing him my credit card, "but it is a fascinating country, and I'm looking forward to my next visit."

Silence.

As he handed me back my credit card and receipt, I asked: "Are there parts of the country that you would recommend if I return?"

"No sir." He turned away quickly and disappeared behind a curtain to an area where his family was now preparing a meal.

My inability to make any connection with this man was disappointing. While I had experienced weeks of distance from my family, my home, and my community, I couldn't imagine how isolated these people must feel after spending their lives in India and then moving to this small, rural Texas town of 1,500 people a few miles from the Mexico border. The culture, the geography, the traditions, the people, the food—all were different. There was seemingly nothing to connect them to the small town of Fort Hancock other than a livelihood.

I headed out on a highway that ran through a number of small farming communities— Acala, Tornillo, Fabens, and Socorro. Pecans were the primary crop in the area; orchards of them, along with fields of alfalfa and onions, painted the landscape. The road ran close to the Rio Grande, which comprised the border with Mexico in this area. As I pedaled, I could look miles to the south and see the Juarez Valley, where Rick, the border patrol agent, had said the Sinaloa and Juarez drug cartels were fighting for power, leaving corpses and frightened citizenry across the land. In the morning newspaper, I had read how the Mexican government had recently flooded the area with thousands of troops to calm the situation. Now, here I was, just a few miles away, alone and safely riding my bicycle and enjoying a warm spring day. A river and a line on a map was the difference. It was strange to consider.

After a few hours of riding, I saw a solitary woman near the town of Acala walking along the edge of a freshly plowed field wearing khakis and a loose fitting T-shirt. As I approached, she beckoned to me with a floppy straw sun hat.

"Excuse me, do you know of a campground nearby that you can recommend?" she asked.

"I don't understand—a campground?"

"A campground. I'm looking for a place for the night."

"I'm still not sure I understand," I said, confused because the woman had no equipment and was walking completely alone.

In response she gave a small laugh and said: "I'm sorry, I should explain."

She introduced herself as Carol and for the next 10 minutes described how she had been traveling the perimeter of the U.S. on foot since 2002, accompanied by her three-legged Pomeranian "Tripod" and a friend, who were both trailing in a support vehicle. The purpose of her walk was to inspire others with handicaps; she then raised her right pant leg to show me her prosthetic leg, which was strikingly decorated with a waving American flag. Carol also wanted to bring to others a message about the value of faith—peace, love, charity, and hope—as opposed to the dictates of any specific religion. I was mesmerized listening to her as she passionately described her goals while completely minimizing all that she had endured over the previous eight years. Finally, after she finished, I pulled out my map and directed her to some possible campgrounds and motels in the area. The encounter was almost surreal. As I said goodbye and rode away I thought that it was not possible to meet someone like Carol, even for just a few minutes, in a remote and dusty field in western Texas and not feel changed by the encounter.

A few miles later, I met a cyclist named Andreas pedaling eastbound from El Paso. He was visiting from the Netherlands and heading to Florida. These occasional encounters with other cyclists were brief, but immensely valuable. We would shake hands, introduce ourselves, and then share information about equipment, road conditions, and places to stay, avoid, and visit, all in the space of a few brief minutes. When Andreas complained about the headwind, it was a reminder for me to get rolling again. It was thrilling to have even a slight breeze at my back after so many days with the wind in my face. My average speed into El Paso that day was three times faster than my ride into Van Horn earlier in the week. The combination of the smooth, flat roadway and tailwind made the day feel effortless. The miles rolled by.

El Paso was a sensory-jarring, 20-mile long strip mall with barbed wire fences, imposing concrete barriers, and walking bridges over the Rio Grande and across the border into Ciudad Juarez. After weeks of staying in small towns, I found that entering a city of 600,000 people overloaded my senses with a riotous landscape of traffic noise, billboards, and flashing lights. I had originally intended to grab a motel in El Paso, but everything felt discordant after the last few days of the desolate beauty of the Texas plains. Plus, I was still feeling strong and had a tailwind. I decided to continue pedaling and a few hours later I reached New Mexico.

Towns in New Mexico have evocative names—Alamogordo, Ruidoso, Mountainair, Truth or Consequences, and Radium Springs—the latter being a small town I passed through that afternoon. Its name made me want to trade my GPS for a Geiger counter, but it was little more than a few trailer homes and abandoned shops. A bit later I rode through the Village of Hatch, which was bigger and had a number of restaurants, grocery stores and roadside stands filled with strands of green, red, and purple dried chiles. Hatch, which is self-proclaimed as the "Chile Capital of the World", is the location of a festival each year that draws thousands of participants and pepper lovers. I was definitely in New Mexico and, by the time I stopped at Caballo Lake for the evening, I had covered over 100 miles for the day and was one state closer to home.

Section 4

Our Hero Finds Solitude in the Saguaro.

(New Mexico, Arizona)

eighteen

Caballo Lake State Park to Silver City, New Mexico
Total Ride Mileage: 2,227

What I thought was a quiet campground at Caballo Lake State Park the previous evening turned out to be pure chaos at dusk when dozens of weekend campers and fishermen arrived almost at once. I was enjoying a dinner of freeze-dried pasta primavera and a beautiful sunset when a crush of RVs descended on the campground from all angles, jockeying for a spot. Diesel engines rapping, gravel crunching, suspensions groaning, wives hollering directions, husbands arguing back. It was a reality show in the making.

At around 9 p.m. things quieted down—or so I thought. An hour later, as I was drifting off to sleep in my sleeping bag, some new neighbors arrived driving two giant diesel 4x4 trucks. One was towing an enormous motor home, the other an oversized barbecue and, behind that, an inflatable pontoon boat. They spent 30 minutes getting unpacked. Then when I thought they were settling in for sleep, they instead cranked up an outdoor karaoke party complete with decorative overhead lighting. The singing went on into the early hours of the morning. I listened to a couple of numbers—they seemed to favor country singers like Toby Keith and Taylor Swift—while looking at the stars and contemplating the state of our fine nation. Then I found my earplugs and jammed them deep into my ears before pulling my sleeping bag over my head, hoping to make it all disappear.

The earplugs worked. I had a surprisingly solid sleep (although I confess to slamming the lid on the trash can nearest my karaoke neighbors early the next morning as a bit of karmic payback). I was rested enough to attempt the

65 miles to Silver City, which would include some of the most challenging hills of my ride. I knew the climbs would test almost every part of my body, but at least my butt would be relatively pain-free because of my saddle.

For some, the term "B-17" brings to mind the fierce "Flying Fortress" bomber used by the U.S. Air Force against Nazi Germany during WWII. For the touring cyclist, however, the term creates a vision not of fear, but rather comfort. Brooks England Ltd. has been making their B-17 leather bicycle saddle for 100 years, and the design has remained almost unchanged. It's cut, shaped, and formed by hand with stainless steel rivets all floating on steel rails. On a modern road bike, it looks as out of place as a Ferrari with running boards. But after a few hundred miles of riding, it softens and molds to your ass like a pair of well-loved jeans. After the weeks of chafing and discomfort at the start of my ride, my saddle was completely broken in. Now, on long, strenuous days of riding, I often imagined some wrinkled, elderly British worker with gnarled knuckles using a wooden mallet and steel anvil to shape my saddle. When I did, I gave quiet thanks to him for his impeccable craftsmanship.

The miles into the town of Hillsboro led through a flat desert, featureless except for an occasional abandoned adobe structure melting from time and the elements like Salvador Dali's pocket watch. It was difficult to imagine people trying to carve out a life in this hard land. Endless miles of scrub and cacti spotted the landscape with not a tree in sight. Yet it was strangely picturesque, reminding me of western author Wallace Stegner's counsel on how to appreciate the special beauty of the desert: "You have to get over the color green. You have to quit associating beauty with gardens and lawns. You have to get used to an inhuman scale."

As I gazed at my surroundings, pedaling in a hypnotic rhythm and lost in contemplative thought, my cell phone rang, abruptly bringing me back to reality. Normally, I turned it off when riding to save the battery, but I must have inadvertently left it on. Coasting to a stop, I fished it out of my pocket.

"Hello," I answered.

"Hi. Is this Mike Dillon?"

"Yes, it is. Who's this?"

"This is Jane Jackson from VMware Corporation. I'm calling because we are considering one of your former employees for a job. I wondered if you have a few minutes to talk and provide a reference?"

Instantly, all of my anxieties crackled to the surface. I should be out finding a job as well. What if I couldn't find one when I returned? How would I explain to my family that I had chosen this ride over my responsibilities to them? What was I doing? Suddenly a quick movement caught my eye. It was a roadrunner darting through the cacti in pursuit of a lizard. I watched for several seconds as they wove through the brush and into the distance. Then I looked up at the beauty of the emptiness around me, the sun shimmering off the blacktop, the miles of olive-gray creosote running to the horizon. I smiled to myself, and said, "Sure. I've got plenty of time."

A few hours later, I stopped in Hillsboro for lunch at the General Store Café. Perhaps it's the striking angle of light at dawn and dusk or its rich cultural diversity, but New Mexico is a lodestone for artists. This town was a good example. Although its population was perhaps 100 and its location 40 miles from any city of note, it had an art school, several art studios, and an artist's co-op store. Like Austin, this community found nourishment in its creative roots as shown by the numerous artists hunched over easels painting different scenes throughout the town.

Leaving Hillsboro, I began a long and windy ride through Percha Canyon and past the town of Kingston, which advertised itself as the home of the Spit & Whittle Club. At the height of the silver boom of the 1890s, Kingston was a thriving town of more than 7,000 citizens. Now its remnants were home to fewer than 30 hearty townsfolk, who lived on a hillside among the pinyon pines, keeping alive one of the nation's oldest continuously meeting social clubs.

After I passed Kingston, I endured a slow and arduous climb over Emory Pass (8,200 ft), taking comfort in the knowledge that some of the world's best cyclists in the Tour of the Gila bicycle race would be riding this same route in a couple of weeks. Scrub oaks, large junipers, and pines lined the road as I climbed toward the pass. Although I occasionally paused to take in the striking views, for the most part I took note of nothing but my fatigue.

At about 7,000 feet, I hit snow (In New Mexico? In April?) and stopped to take a photograph. As I did, a car pulled alongside me. The driver, Will, would have been a middle-aged pirate 200 years ago. Appearing to be in his six-ties, with flowing gray hair, a long drooping mustache, and a bright purple silk headscarf, he fit the part perfectly. He introduced me to his passenger, Sharon, and for the next twenty minutes we discussed my ride. Fortunately, Will was a fellow cyclist from Silver City, and in his sleepy, monotone voice, he offered an overview of what I was going to be facing for the next 40 to 50 miles:

"Maaaannnn, I'm not sure about what you're doing. I've done this ride before without gear, and you still have a long way to go before Silver City."

"Thanks, but I'll be OK. I still have plenty of sunlight left."

"I know maaaaannnn, but it's still a really long way, and you've got plenty of hills after the pass."

"I really appreciate that, but I think I can make it."

"Maaaannnn, I hope so. But, it's a really long way."

"Yeah, I know. Thanks."

"There's also not much water."

"That's OK. I still have water in my bottles."

"And it's pretty remote. Maaaannnn, I don't think this is such a good idea."

And on it went until I finally thanked Will, waved goodbye, and soldiered on.

Twenty minutes later, I reached the summit and discovered Will and Sharon parked there waiting for me. They were sincerely worried that I would not be able to make it to Silver City that evening and offered food and whatever assistance I needed as they tried to convince me to take a ride home with them or to camp for the night near the pass. I was touched by their concern, but stubbornly committed to riding on. Realizing that I wasn't going to change my mind, Will handed me a scrap of paper with his phone number in case I ran into problems; he also doled out specific information about the few remaining water sources and an unmarked place to camp, if needed.

We again parted, and I pedaled on enjoying some wonderful descents, but enduring the torturous additional climbs that Will had described. As the sun started to set, I began to think that perhaps I should have heeded Will's advice. I had covered 30 miles since the pass and was feeling drained as I rode past the Santa Rita copper mine. Only a small portion was visible from the road in the dimming light, but the scale of even this was a challenge to absorb, much less describe. At 1,500 feet deep and 1.5 miles across, Santa Rita is one of the largest open pit mines in the world. Massive dump trucks worked the site, some of which were 25 feet high. Viewed from my vantage point atop the edge of the mine, they looked like little more than a child's Matchbox toys.

Fifteen miles farther, after a day of more than 6,000 feet of climbing, I descended into Silver City. It was dark when I arrived and checked into the first motel I found that was within walking distance of downtown. Before falling asleep, I sent a message to Will and Sharon to thank them for their support and to let them know that they could rest easy. I had made it.

The following morning, I awoke and set off to explore Silver City. A former mining town, it was now a haven for artists of all types. Beautiful murals celebrating the Native American, Hispanic, and Western traditions of the community adorned the walls of the downtown buildings along with contemporary outdoor sculptures. Even the trash bins were decorated with paintings of the blue skies and white cumulus clouds for which the area was renowned. As I walked along the sidewalk, I followed large red painted circles that had been stenciled with the word "Art" to identify studios to visit. The sign on the door of one gallery reinforced the sense that the citizens of Silver City embraced creativity in all aspects of their lives, including the way they ran their businesses:

Hours:
Wednesday thru Saturday 11-4
Sunday, maybe
Monday, possibly
Tuesday, hard to say

Something about the sign struck me. Perhaps it was a legacy of long hours in the regimented cadence of corporate America. All I know is that I would burst out laughing whenever I thought of it.

nineteen

Silver City, New Mexico, to Coal Creek Campground, Arizona
Total Ride Mileage: 2,292

I spent a day of R&R in Silver City enjoying the galleries and the bars and visited a local bike shop for some minor repairs. The respite was needed, and by the next day I was recharged and ready to get back on the road. Pedaling out of town, I climbed a series of small hills that marked the beginning of the Gila River watershed, a system that eventually feeds into the Colorado River. After an hour of riding, I crested a hill that marked the Continental Divide (6,230 ft.). For the next 20 miles, the ride was an easy descent with unobstructed views, no wind, no traffic, just emptiness as far as I could see. Along with coral-shaped buckhorn cholla, dense carpets of Mexican gold poppy, and desert marigolds started to appear along the roadside.

I was reluctant to fully enjoy the long descent because I knew from experience that it would be followed by a climb. To be candid, I was not built for climbing. I have many cycling friends who are, and they all look like whippets with gaunt faces and long limbs. I was better characterized as a Clydesdale. Under the best of circumstances, even without panniers, my climbing cadence is most aptly described as "lumbering," and I did not look forward to the hills ahead.

It took another hour, but I struggled over the climbs, until, at about the 30-mile mark, I noticed a large number of horses crowded together behind a natural windbreak in a large corral and decided to take a breather. As they saw me approach, they lined the fence, greeting me in a surprisingly friendly way. Normally, I don't find animal photographs particularly compelling, especially those taken from a distance. But these were beautiful creatures running around in an inspired setting, and I thought I'd get up close for an interesting picture. Setting down my bike, I calmly approached a brown mare and stroked its head softly, setting up a picture from less than a foot away. The perfect shot, I thought, until the horse made a noise from deep in its throat and forcefully sneezed, coating my forearm, camera, and chest with a nasty slime.

At that moment, I committed that in my future animal photographs the creatures would all appear to be very, very small.

After hundreds of miles of Texas and New Mexico, it wasn't until I approached the community of Buckhorn that I saw my first cowboy on horseback. I had stopped by the side of the road for a pull of water when he trotted by. He was an older, weathered man, wearing the full western outfit of boyhood dreams: tan cowboy hat, denim shirt, red neckerchief, jeans, chaps, and spurs. With a lasso, he flicked at a black cow ambling ahead of him. The era of the cowboy in American history was actually fairly short, lasting only a few decades until the end of the 19th century. What we imagine as the archetypal cowboy is largely a product of Madison Avenue (the "Marlboro Man") and Hollywood (John Wayne in *Red River*), a depiction that is far from reality. Yet when he slowly raised his gloved hand and touched his hat brim to acknowledge me, I couldn't help but feel like a giddy, awestruck eleven-year old watching Sunday morning westerns with my father.

Originally I had planned on staying the evening in the town of Buckhorn at an RV campground that was listed on my map, but when I arrived I could see that it was little more than a dirt parking lot on the edge of the highway. Trying to find an alternative, I stopped at the only store in Buckhorn, Last Chance Pizza Parlor and Liquor, and ordered a pizza as a late lunch while I sat at a table and poured over my map. The only person in the store was Anne, the clerk (and pizza chef), a young woman in her mid-twenties with hennaed hair and tattoos on both arms. She would have better fit at a rave in Manhattan than this sleepy town of fewer than 50 people.

"What's it like living in Buckhorn?" I asked as she took the pizza crust out of the freezer and began unwrapping it.

"It works for me. I've got a good husband and two great kids."

"I don't mean this in the wrong way, but doesn't it get a bit boring at times? There doesn't seem to be a much to do around here if you're young."

"I've had enough of that," she said with a dismissive wave as she started decorating the pizza with cheese and pepperoni. "I lived in the big city, in 'Slowdeatha,' which is what we all call Odessa. It was the wrong place for me. I was hanging out with the wrong people and getting into the wrong things. At some point, I realized my life was going in the wrong direction. So, I called my mom and asked if I could come back home. I think she had her doubts about whether I was ready to settle down, but in the end she said yes. Pretty quickly after that, I met my husband and next thing I know, I'm a mom myself," she said with a giggle. "In the end, I guess a place like Buckhorn was just what I needed."

As I sat eating my pizza, a line from Robert Frost came to mind: "Home is the place where, when you have to go there, they have to take you in." For Anne, that place was Buckhorn.

Ten miles past Buckhorn, the road turned west into the face of another tough headwind exacerbated by the vortex created by the surrounding canyons. Following Anne's directions to a campground, I slowly climbed through the Gila National Forest among an increasing number of pinyon pines and rust-colored rock formations that looked like vertebrae running along the ridgeline. The wind was again a painful distraction. For long stretches, I could not pedal faster than walking speed. More concerning, I was extremely low on water.

At about 60 miles, I passed over the border and into Arizona. It should have been cause for celebration: I had only two states to cover until I was home. But the headwinds had emptied me of any feelings of joy. After climbing a few more tough hills, I finally located a campground Anne had described, leaned my bicycle against a picnic table, stripped off my sweat-soaked jacket, and stalked off in search of water.

I walked to the campground latrine expecting to find a facet nearby, but there was none there or by any of the other campsites. The only other choice was a nearby streambed, which looked to be dry. Walking up it for a few hundred yards, among hoof prints and dung from grazing cattle, I located a few stagnant pools remaining from the last winter rains and filled my bottles, tossing in a few chlorine tablets to help purify the water. I wasn't looking forward to drinking it, but it was better than dehydration, and I knew that boiling the water on my camp stove would kill any remaining nasty critters.

I returned to my campsite with a growing sense of unease. The campground had at least 50 sites, but every one was empty. There wasn't a sign that anyone had been there in months, perhaps, even years. It was giving me a serious case of the creeps. In the last light of the evening, I cooked a quick dinner and got ready for bed, while constantly checking over my shoulder to see if I was still alone.

It reminded me of an evening almost 35 years before. A friend and I had spent the summer driving around the U.S. We were just out of high school with dreams of adventure and travel (and girls), but little money. As a result, the front seats of the car, reeking of teenage sweat and junk food, served as our lodgings on most evenings. One night, after driving late into the darkness and getting lost somewhere in the hills of West Virginia, we decided to grab some sleep and parked in a large, empty gravel lot behind a small elementary school. We reclined the seats and, using our sleeping bags as blankets, fell quickly asleep.

In the middle of night, I was awakened by the crunching of gravel under footsteps and opened my eyes a sliver. Staring in at me, through the other side of the fogged passenger window, I saw the gnarled, battered and partially bloodied face of an older man. It was a scene out of a low-budget horror film. Paralyzed by fright, I remained silent and still until after a few minutes looking into the car the man turned and walked off into the night. My friend slept through everything and doubts my story to this day. But at least he humored me by letting me drive to a safer place to sleep.

This campground had that same kind of desolate, foreboding feel, but I didn't have the security of a traveling companion or a car. I tossed and turned, trying to fall asleep, yet hyper-alert to the sounds around me. Then, as I was cocooned in my sleeping bag under the last traces of twilight and starting to drift off, I saw a large glossy black Lincoln sedan creep slowly into the campground towing a muddy ATV. It was a strange pairing. Why would someone use an expensive luxury car to tow an off-road vehicle? Why would they choose this deserted campground? Why were they arriving in the dark? My mind started to spin out of control. Was this all part of some satanic cult that worshiped by sacrificing middle-aged attorneys traveling alone by bicycle?

After listening to the owner park and begin unpacking in the dark, I decided to face my fear and walk over and introduce myself, praying that I would not encounter a modern version of Norman Bates. Instead, I met Saul, a portly, graying man who appeared to be in his late sixties. He was at first gruff and ill-tempered, but when I volunteered to help him set up a giant Sears, Roebuck and Co. canvas tent that smelled as if it hadn't been out of the box since 1970, he became more sociable.

Saul was from New Jersey but had moved to Florida when he was younger, as he said, "for fear of growing old." In the last decade, he had been dabbling in real estate to support his retirement, and then came the crash of the financial markets in 2008. Saul lost a significant amount of money, and when several of his properties were foreclosed, he decided that he could live more cheaply on the road. He read on the Internet how others had been successful prospecting for gold in the West. So he bought some books on prospecting and took a couple of classes on panning for gold. Then he cashed out his remaining real estate investments and sold most of his possessions, all except for his beloved Lincoln, and bought an ATV and some used camping gear. For the past year, he had been wandering through the remote hills of New Mexico and Arizona, immersing himself in the gold-prospecting culture and hoping that he would find a hidden vein to replenish his lost savings. "Now," he said, "my retirement is going to be spent camping and prospecting—not exactly what I expected at my age." We sat at a picnic table for an hour discussing the recession, real estate, prospecting and our travels, under the glow of his ancient hissing Coleman lantern, until it was time for me to say goodnight. As a parting gift, Saul, having heard me mention my failing water supply, handed me a couple of bottles of water.

Walking back to my campsite I thought about my conversation with Saul. It seems the things we fear most in life are almost always the wrong ones.

twenty

Coal Creek Campground to Globe, Arizona
Total Ride Mileage: 2,365

My alarm clock the next morning was a very garrulous wild turkey. Regretfully, Mother Nature did not create it with a snooze button.

It was the first cold morning in weeks—cold enough that there was a brittle layer of frost covering my ground tarp and bivy sack, causing me to keep refuge in the warmth of my sleeping bag and the thought of further sleep. But this fowl was insistent and kept calling at me from the edge of the woods near my campsite.

Benjamin Franklin had many things right: public libraries, the postal service, his contributions to the U.S. Constitution. However, in one area, he clearly whiffed. That was when he argued to have the wild turkey named as America's national bird. You can only imagine how the Founding Fathers must have responded: "Ben, Ben, we've told you before: It's all about amplifying the U.S.A. brand. We want our 13 colonies to project as more powerful than they are. This means that our national bird can't be one that we eat, or one that chirps, has flashy plumes or a waddle. And, most certainly, no bird that cools itself through urohydrosis!"

What a blow to our national self-esteem if Franklin had his way on this one and we had ended up with the turkey instead of the bald eagle as our national symbol.

Rousting myself out of my bag, I quickly dressed, packed and loaded my gear, while in hushed tones asking the turkey why he couldn't have awakened Saul in his warm, canvas tent instead. Then I headed quietly out of the campsite and started riding through 10 miles of rolling and heavily wooded hills. The exertion quickly warmed me and I had to stop and shed a layer of clothing before climbing through the trees to 6,200 feet in the direction of snow-capped Mt. Graham far to the west. Then, abruptly, the forest ended, and I was staring at the desert valley floor far below. For the next 20 miles, I descended more than 2,000 feet through a series of switchbacks on a smooth roadway with no traffic. Rarely did I tap the pedals. I felt as if I had wings.

Energized by the descent, but cold to the core from the wind chill, I stopped at a market in the town of Three Way and bought a large cup of cowboy coffee and some doughnuts. I ate them on a bench outside enjoying the warmth of the sun penetrating my face and chest. As I relaxed, a middle-aged man with a well-trimmed gray mustache, crisp white shirt, green baseball cap, and Levi's with a knife-edge crease approached and asked about my bike. Dennis had lived in the area all his life. He worked for the Morenci copper mine in nearby Clifton. This was the largest working copper mine in the U.S. (even bigger than the Santa Rita), stretching over 50 square miles. Dennis spent a few minutes explaining the physical and chemical processes associated with copper mining, while I nodded and tried to look engaged. I only wish I had understood a fraction of what he said.

We shared bits of our respective backgrounds, and when I mentioned that I was from a military family, our conversation quickly turned to the subject of patriotism in the U.S. Dennis told me that during the Vietnam War, his small nearby hometown was identified in *Time* magazine as suffering one of the greatest losses of life per capita in the country. He reeled off the names of several of the families he knew that had lost loved ones during the war as if their deaths were a recent event and not from more than 40 years distant. I shared with him how I had observed that almost every hamlet, town, and city I had passed through paid homage to those who had served in the military. It was a common cultural thread that linked the country. As an example, I described something I had seen a few days earlier when I had passed through the town of Valentine, Texas.

Valentine was a forlorn community consisting of dozens of boarded and dilapidated old homes and commercial buildings. There was a library, post office, and one viable business: a mobile home with a sign out front that said "Dental Office." Each February 14th the town's population swelled as temporary workers were hired to apply "Valentine, Texas" postmarks to cards and letters from the amorous. Otherwise, there was little visible employment. Judging by the number of structures, it must have once been a much larger town. Now it could not even support a tavern, market, or gas station. Yet there on the main street was a well-kept memorial encircled by bright new flags; it listed the names of those from the town and surrounding areas that had been killed or were missing in action. This was by no means unique. I'd seen similar memorials, as well as yellow ribbons and POW/MIA flags, in nearly every place I had visited across the country. Some communities even displayed banners or signs listing the names of all their citizens currently on active duty. None of this was a surprise to Dennis. He said that this was just the way one honored true heroes.

For the next few hours after leaving Three Way, I climbed a long, gradual hill on Highway 191 heading toward the town of Safford. After weeks of the muted green, olive, and gray hues of the desert, I was now overwhelmed with waves of color that flowed down the hillsides around me—orange Mexican poppies, pink penstemon, and brilliant red Indian paintbrush. It was startling to see, as if a longtime conservative friend suddenly revealed that she had a large, beautifully colored tattoo.

After reaching the summit, I celebrated another glorious descent extending for several miles, allowing me to marvel at the many floral colors blurring together like a rainbow as I sped by. As I was coasting toward the end of the descent, a cyclist on a heavily loaded touring bike came into view climbing laboriously toward me on the other side of the road. I slowed, waited for a break in the traffic and pulled across the highway to meet him. When I came to a stop he asked, with a pained expression, and not a trace of humor: "When does this get fun?"

"Hi, I'm Mike," I said, shaking his hand.

"Name's Joel. I started from San Diego a week or so ago. Where are you coming from?"

"Jacksonville. I left back in February. I'm heading for the coast and then up to my home near San Francisco."

"Wow, you're on the homestretch!" he exclaimed. Then, after a pause: "So, really, when does this get fun? I'm thinking this is the stupidest fuckin' thing I've ever done. It feels like I'm constantly riding into a headwind, my ass hurts, I haven't found any good places to sleep, and the landscape is painfully monotonous."

Surprised at my own enthusiasm, I found myself trying to give Joel a bit of inspiration. I described the warm-hearted people I had met in the South, the camaraderie of fellow travelers like Don, the inspiring desolation of West Texas, and the sense of independence and freedom I had experienced. Nothing registered in Joel's dull, exhausted eyes. We talked for a few minutes longer about equipment and places to camp.

Then Joel asked, "What am facing for the rest of today?"

"I hate to tell you this, but you have a major climb ahead once you reach the town of Three Way. It was one of the best descents I've enjoyed in over 2,000 miles. So I'm guessing the climb is going to be a challenge. But stick with the ride. Things will get better. I felt the same way as you when I started."

We shook hands and parted. As I rode away, I took one last look over my shoulder at Joel reluctantly mounting his bike. I felt certain that he would never finish his ride.

The next morning, while devastating three pancakes, two eggs, three pieces of bacon, three pieces of sausage, a mountain of hash browns, and four cups of coffee at a small diner, I received a message from Don, who had been trailing a day behind me. He indicated that he was thinking of staying the evening at a hot spring called Essence of Tranquility and suggested that I meet him there. Given my sore muscles, the words "hot spring" would have motivated me to do damned near anything, and I told Don that I'd meet him there later in the day.

I did a quick bit a research and located the hot spring only about 10 miles away down a series of narrow dirt roads. It's a difficult place to describe, although the name certainly provides some clues. Think 1968, crystals, incense, tie-dye, and aromatherapy, and you get an idea. The grounds consisted of several cabins and camping sites adjacent to five small pools fed by a natural hot spring. The proprietors offered not only the hot spring, but also touch therapy, reflexology, and something called ear coning. (I was too frightened to ask what the latter was, but I suspected it played a key part in the Star Trek movie

Wrath of Khan.) There was also a large communal kitchen and living room with TV and Wi-Fi.

Waiting for Don to arrive, I ended up spending the day like this:

Soak in hot springs.
Read book.
Nap in shade.
Repeat.

Don eventually rolled in toward the late afternoon, and we enjoyed a dinner of soup and salad while comparing stories from our travels since last camping together. Our meal was accompanied by shots of medicinal agave juice (i.e. tequila) carried in my panniers for emergencies (which were becoming a nightly occurrence) and an abundance of cervezas hauled in Don's trailer. I thought the combination of food, drinks, a day soaking in the hot spring, and the healing power of crystals and incense would lead to a good night's sleep. Instead, the sounds of coyotes, donkeys, roosters, and dogs frequently interrupted my slumber. Each time I awoke, I looked overhead from my sleeping bag and tracked the progress of the night by the movement of Ursa Major overhead. Finally, at first light, I gave up, packed, said a quiet goodbye to Don, and headed off.

I traveled for much of the day through the San Carlos Apache Indian Reservation, a nearly 3,000-square-mile reservation in southeast Arizona. It was here that I encountered my first menacing dog in weeks. It was an extremely large Rottweiler that barked and snarled, sprinting alongside me on the opposite side of the highway. Given his size, around 80 to 100 pounds, I would normally have been confident that I could outride him; however, on this particular morning, I mistakenly chose to enjoy the "Lumberjack Slam" at a Denny's restaurant after leaving the hot springs and was feeling extremely bloated when the dog made his charge. This was a most intimidating animal and, as I jumped on the pedals, I grew worried that my lucky streak would end. With my pulse racing, I quickened my cadence as the dog stalked me across the highway, attempting to dart between breaks in the traffic to get at me. Fortunately, my canine karma held; the dog was blocked from crossing the highway by a succession of oncoming trucks, and I was able to successfully make my escape.

In the town of Fort Thomas, I took a break at a local store that was another one of those fascinating establishments that attempted to satisfy all local consumer desires; it sold one of every item, from live minnows to used tires to rifles to stuffed rattlesnakes to nail guns to VCR movies to birthday cakes. It also had an adjoining gas station, mini-mart, and restaurant.

A few miles farther, I stopped in the town of Bylas when I noticed several cars parked in a dirt lot with hand-lettered cardboard signs that said "Food Sale." One of them offered a favorite of mine: Indian fry bread. I coasted to a stop alongside the car, a beat-up 1970s station wagon. As I straddled my bike, I smiled at the middle-aged woman sitting in the front seat and said: "I love fry bread. The last time I had it was in Montana. Can I get two, please?"

She gave no response, other than a momentary look of contempt, as she reached into a plastic box on the back seat. Handing me two hand-wrapped aluminum packages, she said in a monotone voice, "Two bucks."

I handed her the money and quickly started eating.

"These are very good."

No reply.

"How long have you lived in Bylas?"

Nothing.

"Beautiful scenery through this area."

Silence.

"What do you think of President Obama's proposal for a single-payer health care system?"

In response, she turned to stare at me with a face as expressive as an Easter Island moai, but said not a word.

I'd heard from other cyclists that the people on this reservation were not receptive to visitors, and I certainly got a sense of it that day. In every town where I stopped on the reservation, I was invisible. People walked past, avoided eye contact, and were laconic in response to my questions, if they replied at all. While disappointing, it wasn't a surprise as it was a reflection of the treatment Native Americans had received for centuries and I was an outsider.

I continued through the desert for 50 miles. In the cool morning air lizards warming themselves on the asphalt shot away from my wheels like sparks on the roadway. The colorful wildflowers continued their exhibition with yellow marigolds, white daisies, purple lupine, and sage surrounding me.

As I started the climb toward the communities of Peridot and Globe, I saw my first saguaro of the trip. It was a large one, approximately 15 feet high, with arms outstretched to the sky. By the end of the day, these surrounded me like silent soldiers of the desert. Almost as omnipresent were memorials for those killed in traffic accidents on this stretch of the highway. They came in the form of crucifixes made out of wood, rebar, PVC pipe, ceramics, or plastic. In some places, three or four crosses were grouped together, indicating the loss of an entire family. Many were decorated with wilting Mylar balloons, plastic garlands, dried flowers, or they contained offerings to the dead—a personal note, an empty shot glass, a stuffed animal, an unopened can of beer. They were at once heartening and haunting.

But, mainly haunting.

twenty one

Globe to Paradise Valley, Arizona
Total Ride Mileage: 2,588

Forget Jenny Craig, Slim-Fast, or other weight-loss aids. Riding long distances on a fully loaded touring bike is an extremely effective way to lose the middle-aged spread. Often I burned 5,000-6,000 calories during a full day of riding. As a consequence, food as fuel was a constant focus. When I left Globe the following morning, my thought was to make it a short day and detour up Highway 188 to visit the archeological ruins of Tonto National Monument and camp somewhere nearby. Assuming that breakfast would be my only real meal of the day, I stopped at a café, took a look at the menu, and ordered one of almost everything from the breakfast section. The amount I was eating was astounding. Even more concerning was the pace at which I ate. Hunger overtook etiquette at most meals and, as I was wolfing down my breakfast, I was certain I overheard my waitress speaking to another about the possibility of installing a spark arrestor on my fork.

The ride to Tonto National Monument was a gradual climb to 3,800 feet followed by a beautiful, leisurely descent toward Theodore Roosevelt Lake. The only blemish on the wondrous scenery was the hundreds of Harley-Davidson motorcycles rolling past me. There must have been a biker rally nearby because they were everywhere and annoying as hell.

I had been looking forward to visiting Tonto. I saw on my map that it had a well-preserved pair of cliff dwellings built by the Salado people, and I was interested in seeing how these compared to the Anasazi ruins I had explored during past trips to Utah. Unfortunately, after an extremely steep ride up to the visitor center, I arrived to find that the sites were closed due to an invasion of Africanized (aka "killer") bees, and the cliff dwellings could only be viewed from a remote distance through a spotting scope.

I was discouraged, especially after the miles I had put into the detour to visit this site. Trying to make the best of things, I asked a ranger about camping sites in the area or along a desolate and infrequently used dirt roadway known as the Apache Trail.

"You aren't thinking of riding that on a bicycle, are you? You mean a dirt bike—as in a motorcycle?" he responded.

"No, I'm on a bicycle."

"I've never heard of anyone doing that. I guess it could be done, but it's dirt for almost 30 miles. Occasionally someone in a 4x4 uses it, but not often. It's really not much of a road and is often washed out in the spring."

The conversation with the ranger gave me little confidence about taking the trail route. However, as I left the ranger station, a local resident started talking to me as I was standing by my bike looking at a map. I used the opportunity to ask him about the idea of riding the Apache Trail. Before responding, he asked me a number of questions about my ride, including how many miles I'd ridden each day and which mountains I'd climbed. Then he said, "Son, I think you can do it."

With a split vote, I rode to the local National Forest Service office and spoke with one of the rangers. While she said she couldn't advise me whether it was safe, she did have a binder with aerial photographs of the Apache Trail, and she identified a number of places where camping was possible along the way. I pedaled off, drawn by the idea of an adventurous detour, but concerned about a breakdown on a desolate desert road. Then a stream of "brappping" Harleys riding past made the decision for me. I would take my chances on the Apache Trail rather than listen to them all day.

A few miles past the ranger station, I pulled off the highway and onto the Apache Trail; the road abruptly changed from asphalt to dirt. Although the surface had at some time in the distant past been graded, the dirt was now soft and inches deep, masking rocks hidden beneath that I worried would damage my wheels. It would be a terrible place to snap a rim. At the base of some small descents, the road would washboard, causing vibrations that I could feel in my molars. I quickly learned to slow down well in advance of these washes (where sand covers the road after flooding). When I hit those at speed, I felt as though I was trying to ride on ice; my forearms burned as I wrestled to keep the bike vertical. An additional irritation was a few raised SUVs and 4x4 trucks that drove by using the trail for off-roading. As they passed, I glanced through the windows to see their passengers slurping down Big Gulps and staring at me as if I were a zoo animal. None had the sense to slow down, leaving me coughing and coated in dust as they sped by.

But around every corner was a new visual delight. The trail ran through a series of canyons with small reservoirs and lakes that eventually fed water to the greater Phoenix area. With towering monoliths and multi-colored layers of sandstone beside the deep blue of the water, it looked like a smaller version of the Grand Canyon. And, after the vehicles had disappeared, for long stretches I felt as if it were all mine. Clearly, the local inhabitants were not expecting me. I would turn a corner and cause cottontail rabbits and Gambel's quail to scatter or a coati to seek protection in the brush. Bright crimson-flowered beaver-tail cacti appeared along with enormous saguaros and whip-like ocotillos—all against the backdrop of the slow-moving water below.

I was intoxicated by the scenery; flooded with an overwhelming sense of warmth and well-being. I had experienced this euphoria before when camping beside granite-framed lakes in the High Sierra or while kayaking in the remote reaches of northern Canada. Engaging with nature in quiet solitude tunes the spirit to its primordial past. It helps us to find balance in our increasingly harried lives and nourishes something within that has long been forgotten. On that day, I felt that connection. And it grew in intensity as I pedaled.

As the sun began to set, the foliage of the canyons became shades of green that I had never seen before or even thought possible, all of them accented with the rust, umber, and salmon hues of the fading light on the sandstone walls. Two miles east of Tortilla Flat, the dirt trail abruptly returned to an asphalt road. I continued past a campground there and another one a few miles further at Canyon Lake, lost in my reverie and in the beauty of the mountains silhouetted against the afterglow of sunset. Still I kept pedaling. To the north, stars began to appear above Weaver's Needle, a craggy rock formation that had served as a landmark for a century of treasure hunters searching for the legendary fortunes of the Lost Dutchman Mine. Venus rose near the sliver of the moon, and coyotes mournfully wailed in the darkness. I coasted through sage-scented air at the bottom of each hill in a state of near rapture, until, finally, my energy ebbed, and I knew that even days as sublime as this must come to an end.

In contrast to the desolate beauty of the previous day, after departing from my campsite the next morning I spent most of the day threading crowded Phoenix roadways to the place where I would be staying for the next few days, the home of some longtime friends in nearby Paradise Valley. This was one of flattest urban areas that I had ever visited. Instead of growing vertically as the population increased, Phoenix had expanded horizontally into the surrounding desert. In fact, the area we refer to as "Phoenix" is actually a combination of 22 cities (including Mesa, Gilbert, Tempe, Chandler, Scottsdale, Paradise Valley, Phoenix, and Peoria) that have coalesced under the ceaselessly expanding population of nearly 1.8 million people. The urban sprawl of the area seemingly had no end.

Navigating the traffic and streets was made more challenging by the thousands of runners in bright T-shirts participating in "Pat's Run." Pat Tillman was a former college and NFL football star who walked away from a multi-million dollar professional football contract to enlist in the Army Special Forces at the beginning of the war in Iraq. On a subsequent deployment in Afghanistan he was killed by friendly fire, an outcome that the military administration attempted to cover up. For the government, portraying Tillman as a war hero lost in battle with the enemy offered a better narrative for recruiting posters. They didn't, however, consider the Tillman family who, through doggedness and determination, brought the truth to light. Then the family did something even more remarkable; they started a series of programs at colleges around the country in Tillman's name focused on ethical leadership. Organized fun runs such as the one around me funded these programs. Stopping on a corner, I watched participants stream by, a confluence of diverse ages, cultures, and political views, all united for a common purpose. I thought back to my conversation with Dennis near the town of Three Way a few days earlier. I knew that he would have agreed that this was a demonstration of American patriotism at its best.

I arrived in Paradise Valley late in the afternoon, where my friends Rob and Marian welcomed me with wonderful hospitality beginning with a mouth-watering steak dinner and a bottle of delicious red wine. After weeks of eating on picnic benches out of an aluminum camping bowl or from paper plates at fast food restaurants, sitting at a comfortable table and relaxing over a meal with two long-time friends made me almost teary-eyed with happiness.

While Rob and Marian were at work the following day, I used the time to relax, to chart the remaining miles home, and to attend to some repairs on my bike. While cleaning it, I had noticed a wobble in the front tire and took it to a bicycle shop in Scottsdale, thinking that the wheel needed to be realigned. The mechanic took the wheel apart and explained that the problem was that the cone and bearings were grooved. He advised me that the wheel would not complete the ride unless it was repaired. He also explained that he would need to order the replacement parts, which would take at least a week to arrive. Because I needed to get back on the road in a matter of days, I tried another place, but with the same result. In desperation, I went to a much smaller shop, also located in Scottsdale. When I arrived I found Brad, the head mechanic, sitting behind the counter, munching on a giant Subway sandwich. After I explained my predicament, he admitted that he also didn't have the parts in stock. But noting the look of dejection on my face, he said: "Hang out for a bit while I finish up my lunch, and I'll see if I can think of another solution."

As he chewed his sandwich, Brad asked about my route and gear, and I quickly discovered that he and his girlfriend had also finished a cross-country ride the previous year. They had started in Oregon and traveled across Idaho, Montana, and around the Great Lakes, ending in New York. While he was eating, we compared experiences, and then, after he was finished, he disappeared into the storeroom and returned with a wheel and began to disassemble it. With a conspiratorial grin, he confided that it was from his manager's bicycle, but explained that he was out of town, and Brad would order the parts and replace them before his boss returned. After a few minutes he had successfully removed the parts and installed them in my wheel, greased, and then reassembled it. When I asked what I owed him, he waved me off: "When I did my ride, many people helped me. I'm just doing the same, just passing it on."

Surprise should have been my reaction, but it wasn't. Over the many weeks of riding, I had discovered and joined a fraternity of touring cyclists. Its members provided information, food, parts, repairs, and, on occasion, commiseration—with little expectation of return other than the reward of helping others who were seeking, as Joni Mitchell once sang, the "refuge of the roads."

twenty two

Paradise Valley to Wickenburg, Arizona
Total Ride Mileage: 2,650

Rob and Marian were wonderful company. Three nights in a comfortable bed had done much to improve my disposition and to prepare for the final push home. It also allowed me to reunite with a longtime friend.

"Johnny Drama," nicknamed for his resemblance to a character from the TV show *Entourage*, had been a friend of mine since high school. I had asked a number of friends to join me for part of the ride, but all had excuses—most of them pretty weak ones. Drama, however, came through. Over the previous decades, we had enjoyed kayak trips in Canada and other assorted adventures together, and now he was looking for a break from his job as a financial advisor in the midst of one of the worst economic downturns of the last 100 years. He had been monitoring my progress as I pedaled west, and, despite having little cycling experience, decided to meet me in Phoenix and accompany me through the remainder of Arizona and into California. Late in the evening on my last day in Paradise Valley, Drama arrived from the airport, hauling an old mountain bike retrofitted with road bike tires, a new trailer loaded with gear, and a mind brimming with apprehension about traffic, road conditions, weather, and, above all else, my directional abilities.

Drama and I departed Paradise Valley the next morning at dawn. As we rode off, he quietly confided, "Mike, there are two things I haven't done yet: learned how to correctly pack my trailer or learned how to ride with it." Despite this inexperience, he gave a strong effort, covering the day's more than 60 miles with little difficulty, except for a flat tire near the town of Wittmann.

It was a tough day for cycling: sweltering hot and far from scenic. It took us almost two hours to exit the urban sprawl surrounding downtown Phoenix. From there, we traveled through miles of road construction and the towns of Glendale, Sun City, El Mirage, and Surprise, all of which undoubtedly will someday become part of the Phoenix metropolitan area.

Drama was new to distance cycling, and, like many middle-aged neophytes embarking on an unknown activity, he had spared no expense on his equipment. He was a vision of neon yellow—jersey, shoes, water bottle, and trailer bag—making him visible for miles. That's great for safety, but not for the guy following close behind. To avoid retinal damage, I wisely rode in front for much of the day.

Near the town of Surprise, we pedaled past a Costco-like superstore called "Guns Plus," dedicated to all manner of firearms, ammunition, and shooting supplies. As I peered through the window, I wondered what it is in the American psyche that is so irrational when it comes to gun regulation. More than 30,000 of our fellow citizens die each year from firearm violence at rates more than 10 times that of any other industrial nation. Yet, year after year, tragedy after tragedy, the country is unable to unite around any sensible regulation. For example, it's estimated that more than 40 percent of all annual gun sales are made without background checks, often at gun shows and through private transactions. But legislative attempts to change this consistently fail. On the other hand, a rigorous background and reference check were required for a friend of mine to lead a spinning class at his local YMCA. As Americans, firearm deaths are acceptable, but clearly we can't tolerate anyone pulling a hamstring at the hands of a crazed spinning instructor.

As we pedaled south of Wickenburg, I pointed to a hand-painted sign on a large rundown wooden building that said "Hank's–Open Dayley," [sic], and Drama and I pulled over for a quick stop. Upon entering, we were greeted by the owner of Hank's Antique Store, who was not named Hank, but rather Omar. He appeared to be in his late eighties and was dressed in a threadbare flannel shirt and worn black slacks held up by a set of wide suspenders. As we wandered his shop amid piles of dust, junk, and treasure, Omar trailed us as though we were his first customers.

Omar grew up as a local boy and spent his early adulthood selling cars in a local dealership during the 1940s and 50s. When the nearby Vulture Mine opened, he changed jobs for a higher paying career mining for a mineral called galena. Many years later, after spending decades as a pack rat, buying things at garage and estate sales, he decided to retire and run this shop. Neither Drama nor I had heard of galena previously, which motivated Omar to give us a very enthusiastic tutorial on the wonders of this mineral, including a demonstration of how Guglielmo Marconi had used galena crystals in the first transistor radio.

Perhaps it was in gratitude for the enthusiasm of his stories (our quick break had turned into almost an hour), but I felt obliged to purchase something from Omar and chose the first thing that hit my eye: an old commemorative Indiana State porcelain plate, as a gift for Liz from the state where she was born. It wasn't the brightest of choices given that I had no idea how I was going to keep it unbroken in my panniers for 700 more miles, but clearly I was growing confident in my ability to avoid an accident. I just hoped I wouldn't get cocky and at a future stop purchase a matching set of Waterford crystal.

We reached our destination of Wickenburg in the mid-afternoon. Wickenburg was home to the Desert Caballeros Western Museum, a small but impressive museum that included a large collection of chaps, spurs, ropes, saddles, and historical artifacts, as well as a special exhibit showing the works of female western artists. One of the docents, Bob Joyden, gave us a personal tour of the museum's extensive display of bola ties. It's the tie of choice for every politician or celebrity who wants to demonstrate his link to the West. Bob explained that one of the town's residents, Vic Cedarstaff, had invented the bola in the 1940s. According to local lore, while Cedarstaff was riding his horse one day, his hat flew off, leaving only the rawhide band, which he placed around his neck for safekeeping. Later, a group of his friends teased him about his unique tie—and history was made.

That evening, as I sat outside the motel room enjoying the warm evening breeze and a moment of solitude to write in my journal, an elderly, extremely drunk, bow-legged cowboy staggered in my direction and turned toward the door of the hotel room next to me. He leaned against the doorway and repeatedly tried to insert his key in the lock without success. With each attempt, he would burst into ever more boisterous laughter. Suddenly noticing my presence, he said something that sounded like, "havin'g mumble mumble with ma door key mumble mumble," delivering a loud belch as a coda. Then he shakily flopped down into a metal chair next to me, shook my hand, and introduced himself as "Chuck."

Given that I was sober at the time, I struggled to understand Chuck. His lingua franca was liquor, and with his mumbling, slurring, and occasional fits of laughter, I could do little at first but nod my head and look interested. However, after a bit of time, I tuned into Chuck's unique speech pattern and was able to translate.

"Jistgot paid 'ay." ("I just received my paycheck today.")

"Oh?"

"Yup. Jisgot paid, z'ts y I'mma 'ere," ("Yes. I was just compensated for my work. It's the reason I'm in town.")

"What do you mean? Do you work here?"

"Nononononono. I urk onn'a rnch. Cominta town 'ice a mnth anna I git ma chk and blow offa lettle steam." ("No, I don't. I work as a hand at a local ranch. I visit town twice a month when I get paid to enjoy some fine dining, entertainment, and local culture.")

He pointed at the hotel. "Ushulee ah sthayere." ("When I'm in Wickenburg, I prefer to stay at this wonderful establishment.")

Then, after a brief pause, he broke into rowdy laughter: "Jis got thrown outta ma 'rd bar tahnght, stil'ave summa 'ney eft!" ("I was just asked to leave from a third drinking establishment this evening because I was not acting appropriately; however, I have not yet spent all of my remaining salary.")

Then he leaned toward me, slapped my knee and said, "Wanna go'ith me n triffora frrth?" ("Would you like to accompany me to a fourth drinking establishment to see if I will again be asked to leave?") At this, he burst into uproarious laughter.

I told Chuck that while I appreciated the invitation, I had to decline because I had a big day of riding ahead of me. Then, I watched as he finally managed to get the door open, staggered to his room, and launched face-forward onto his bed completely passed out. As I listened to his snoring, I looked up at the star-filled skies, marveling at the characters of the West.

After writing a few more pages in my journal, I decided that I should follow Chuck's lead and get some sleep. I quietly turned off the light in his room, shut the door and headed off to bed, knowing that Drama and I still had a bit of a problem we needed to solve in the morning. Drama, who had spent hundreds of dollars on the latest in chic riding apparel, had neglected to think about one minor item in preparing for this trip: his tires. The previous day, when changing his flat, I noticed that the rubber beads affixed to the wheel rim were disintegrating. Looking more closely, I discovered that his tires dated back to shortly after Charles Goodyear first vulcanized rubber. I lined the inside with some duct tape (don't leave home without it) to strengthen the weaker portions of the tire wall, but it was questionable how long it would last, especially in the heat of the desert.

Because there were no bicycle stores for more than 40 miles, the next morning we walked to the town hardware store but were unsuccessful in finding a replacement tire. We were about to try the local thrift store in the hope that it had a used bike with the size tire we needed, when I saw a slender man sitting on a bench in front of city hall with a mountain bike propped next to him. He introduced himself as Louis and confirmed that there was no place in town to buy a tire, but he recalled that he might have an old bicycle at home with the same size as we needed and said that he would ride home and get it for us.

Thirty minutes later, there was a knock on our motel room door. There stood Louis, holding out a wheel. "Knew I had it," he said. "It's off an old junker that I haven't ridden for years."

I invited him into the room while I stripped the tire off the wheel and installed it onto the rim of Drama's bike. As I was doing this, Louis told us that he was a former business executive from Southern California who, six years ago, had discovered religion and quit his job to become a pastor. He now operated a window washing business to raise money for his ministry, and his only form of transportation was his bicycle. With a trailer towing Bibles and cleaning supplies, he traveled throughout the area washing office windows, providing religious instruction, and raising money for the poor and homeless.

Louis wouldn't take payment for the tire, but we finally convinced him to accept a donation for his ministry before he left. As we were packing our gear for the ride to Salome, Drama spoke excitedly about Louis's generosity, amazed that a stranger would go home, remove a tire from his old bicycle, and bring it to a couple of strangers at their hotel with no thought of personal gain. I smiled and thought of Brad, the mechanic in Scottsdale, Don, Jan, and the other riders I had met over the previous months and said: "Welcome to the brotherhood of touring cyclists."

twenty three

Wickenburg, Arizona, to Blythe, California
Total Ride Mileage: 2,767

The following morning, Drama and I rode quietly for several hours, working our way through a mesquite-filled desert under brooding skies and dappled sunlight. The moisture in the air released the fragrance of the many spring blooms, enhancing the dramatic vista around us. As we turned to the southwest, however, the headwinds increased and the temperature plummeted quickly, convincing us to stop at the Coyote Flats Café in Aguila (pop. 1,000) for a green chili hamburger and, more importantly, warmth. While waiting for our food and rubbing our frozen limbs to regain circulation, I looked around the restaurant and noticed several posters advertising a local triathlon. Given the small size of the community, I wondered about the number of participants and distances for the event. As I read more closely, it turned out that this "triathlon" consisted of these three events: horseshoes, pool, and darts.

And, who says Americans don't exercise enough?

Adjacent to the café was a motel with a well-worn sign atop a tall pole in front of it. Unlike the signs in front of urban hotels, which are frequently replaced in their entirety when new room amenities are offered, in small towns it is more common to keep the old sign and update it. For example, a sign for a small-town Mississippi motel where I had stayed advertised "ceiling fans," then further down the pole: "refrigerated rooms," and further still, "air conditioning." Similarly, in Alabama, one motel sign promoted "Color T.V." (with the letters spelled in different colors), then "Satellite T.V.," and finally "Wi-Fi." These motel signs were a fascinating modern equivalent of the totem pole, telling the story of the last century's technological advances.

As we left the restaurant, I received a call from Don in response to a message I had left earlier in the day. The tire that Louis gave Drama was serviceable but worn, and I had asked Don, who was now riding ahead of us near Blythe, California, if there were any bicycle stores in the area. Don told me that he had located a bicycle shop there and confirmed that they had the right size in stock should we need it. Don and I had previously discussed meeting again and riding together up the coast of California, but as we spoke, he told me that he had changed his mind and decided to finish by going directly to San Diego. From there he was going to fly home to Alaska and either "pick up some construction work" or "drive his truck to New York to visit family." As we said our goodbyes and hung up, I felt a surprising sense of sadness, knowing that Don and I would not again enjoy a beer-fueled exchange of stories under a star-filled night on this trip. My periodic encounters with Don had helped to stave off loneliness—not to mention teaching me to use a toilet as a wine chiller. Somewhere along the last 3,000 miles, I had made a good friend, and I knew that I would see his gap-toothed grin on a future journey.

Drama and I cycled through a handful of small communities that day before we reached Salome. In one town, we passed a red cinder block tavern displaying the ultimate example of truth in advertising: "Hot Beer, Lousy Food, Bad Service." Most of the ride, however, was less amusing—a relentless push into the wind. In some places the wind spawned large dust devils rising high into the air that were visible for miles. For much of the day, Drama was stoic and I sensed he was questioning what I had gotten him into.

The following morning, we quietly rode out of Salome under cold, gray skies and intermittent rain. Along the way, we passed through the very small town of Hope. In fact, the only indication that a town existed was a sign that announced, "Hope, Arizona," and then a few hundred yards later another one that said, "Your [sic] now beyond Hope." As with patriotism, this type of small town humor, much of it self-deprecating, was a unique attribute of our national personality that I saw displayed often as I pedaled across the country.

Through the grey morning haze we travelled slowly past a collection of buttes and mesas set against a jagged mountain backdrop. The scenery resembled those silhouetted paintings of the Southwest that you see at local art festivals. I found intense beauty in the sparseness. For much of the ride, I held back and let Drama travel far ahead so that he could enjoy the experience of riding alone through the desert. In this era of constant personal connectivity, where everyone is linked to MP3 players, mobile phones, iPads, and social networking sites, this sense of solitude is a rarity.

An hour after passing through Hope, a lone figure appeared on the horizon. As we drew closer, we saw that it was a cyclist who a few minutes later pulled over to speak with us. It was an unexpected encounter, like meetings between early American mountain men who infrequently crossed paths. There was no sign of life as far as the eye could see—just three people on bicycles meeting by chance on a solitary road in an endless expanse of desert.

Neil was riding his bicycle to Gainesville, Florida, after a tour across the northern U.S. the previous year. He was riding extremely light and fast, with only two small saddlebags of gear. His sole focus was on mileage and speed, since he was trying to cross the country as quickly as possible, averaging between 100 and 125 miles per day. He had planned his ride with logistical precision so that he could sleep in a motel each night and eliminate the need for camping gear. As we spoke, I sensed his impatience to be in motion again. After two months wandering the country, I was puzzled by his desire to cover it so fast. Decades of my life, primarily those associated with "The Job," had been spent in the regular cadence of work life: completing projects, working on department budget reviews, setting annual plans, managing cases, negotiating transactions, implementing new processes, and an endless succession of scheduled meetings. Now it was liberating to let the weather, my surroundings, and interests dictate my course each day. I was finding immense joy in the freedom and lack of structure.

Passing through the small town of Brenda, Drama and I were surrounded by an enormous RV park with hundreds of vehicles joining together each year to form a community in the middle of the desert. When we stopped there for a bite to eat, I listened to the conversations around me. There was a couple from Chicago who drove down each spring towing a jeep so that they could go off-roading in the desert, a man from New York who visited annually for the warm weather, a group of retired friends who enjoyed doing nothing except grilling meat and drinking beer. Despite the interesting people, I found most RV parks like this one to be bleak places to stay. Lying on my sleeping bag contemplating the evening sky overhead, while sandwiched between large cylinders of steel with blaring televisions and gas-powered generators was not the experience I had imagined for this ride. But RV parks were sometimes the only available place to camp.

For some, they were the only option as well, but for different reasons. In many places, I met families who now called these locations "home" as the result of a major financial misfortune—a lack of health insurance, a home foreclosure, or the loss of employment. Sometimes, as I packed my gear in the morning, I would see young children stepping from their trailers or RVs and walking to a school bus stop, toting lunch bags and school backpacks. This stark illustration of the gap between the "haves" and "have-nots" was always a depressing way to start the day. Each time I witnessed it, I thought how a cross-country bicycle ride should be required for all members of the U.S. Congress.

A few miles past Brenda, we merged onto the I-10 freeway. Riding on the interstate was an entirely new and adrenalin-depleting experience. Although the shoulder was wide and smooth, it was filled with terrestrial flotsam: broken bottles, used diapers, plastic water bottles, fast food bags and wrappers. A bigger obstacle was the shredded tire treads of 18-wheelers; they slithered like black snakes across the roadway. Navigating this roadway, especially when going downhill, presented unexpected challenges, as did the trucks speeding by only a few feet from my shoulder. Their high-pitched drone sounded like a turn at the Indianapolis 500 and I was constantly buffeted by their slipstream as they passed only a few feet away.

In the mid-afternoon, after spending several successful hours without becoming road kill on I-10, I crossed the bridge over the Colorado River and into California. As a joke, Drama took a photograph of me prostrating myself and kissing the roadway in front of the "Welcome to California" sign. But I would be lying if I didn't admit to choking down my emotions.

I felt like I was almost home.

Section 5

Our Hero Discovers That He Still Has Far to Travel
Before He Is Home.

(California)

twenty four

Blythe to Yucca Valley, California
Total Ride Mileage: 2,767

The next day we continued on I-10 wrestling with more than 60 miles of long haul trucks, mobile homes, and campers until we finally exited the freeway and made the seven-mile climb into Joshua Tree National Park, our destination for the night. When we arrived at our campsite, we were completely depleted from the traffic, heat and climb, but it was too early to turn in. Instead, after a shower and freeze-dried dinner, Drama and I walked down to the small campground amphitheater and listened to a ranger give a presentation about a day in the life of the Cahuilla Indians, who lived in this area 1,000 years ago. It was a surprisingly lively talk that managed to keep us awake until nightfall. While speaking about the local fauna, the ranger informed us that the scorpions in Joshua Tree were nocturnal; if we wanted to catch one, we'd need to place a piece of red plastic over our flashlight, because they couldn't see the color red. This piece of information left me with two questions: Who carries around a piece of red plastic while camping? And, more importantly: Why would anyone want to catch a scorpion?

I awoke the next morning from a terrible sleep, not because of the scorpions, but because of the campground's other nocturnal activity. A bit past midnight, one fellow camper decided to entertain a group of friends with his guitar. He was quite a talented musician who covered everything from jazz to blues to country. But I needed rest more than a concert.

Using my earplugs, I managed to fall back asleep until 4 a.m. That's when I was awakened by a couple in a nearby RV, *in flagrante delicto*. It was a loud, lengthy, and energetic session, evidently filled with religious fervor ("Oh, Jesus! Oh, Jesus!"). If I hadn't been so tired, I would have walked over to their rig and given them a big round of applause for such a committed performance and even used my lighter to request an encore. Instead, I buried my laughter in my sleeping bag and fell back asleep for several more hours.

The next morning, Drama and I enjoyed our last meal together and then he headed south toward Palm Springs, where his wife was going to pick him up. In his week riding with me, he had experienced almost everything—rain, heat, dust, mechanical failures, and questionable accommodations—everything except a dog attack. But at least he had something to look forward to when I invited him on a future ride. While I had enjoyed Drama's company, on reflection, I realized that I preferred the solitude of riding alone. Like most adults, as I had grown older, I had become increasingly responsible for others: family, friends, and co-workers. To be accountable only for myself was a pleasure I had long missed. When I awakened each morning, my only concern was where I would rest that evening. Every other decision was made as the day progressed and was based on my desire for food, entertainment, or exploration (and headwinds), rather than on the needs of others. Perhaps this was selfish, but after years in the corporate world, I had begun to treasure this time alone.

Despite the lack of sleep, I was excited about the day's ride since I would be traversing famous Joshua Tree National Park from south to north. For five hours, with the exception of a handful of tourist-filled automobiles, I enjoyed its unique beauty in solitude. After a short initial climb, the route turned into a long slow descent into the Pinto Basin. Yellow-flowered creosote bushes lined the horizon along with crimson-tipped ocotillo, dune evening primrose with their long white tubular blossoms and cholla cactus looking as if they were from another galaxy. Speeding down the mountain, I passed gravel service roads running to the horizon like pale dirt contrails across the desert floor.

As I climbed the 1,600 feet out of Wilson Canyon, I finally saw the plant for which the park was named. This tree is a species of yucca that was christened with the name Joshua tree by Mormon settlers because its upright branches were seen by some to resemble the waving arms of the Old Testament prophet Joshua as he pointed toward the Promised Land. In an interesting bit of symbiosis, the Joshua tree is only pollinated by the female pronuba moth, which in turn lays its eggs in the tree's flowers so that the moth larvae can later feed on the yucca's seeds. One can't survive without the other.

This co-dependency was something I found that I shared with my bicycle. Neither of us could move effectively without the other and it had become more than just a mode of transportation. On some nights, while I cooked dinner in some remote campground, I would find myself quietly talking to my steel and rubber companion, sharing plans for the coming day as if it could hear me. Frequently, I would look at the map under the light of my lantern and marvel at how far we had carried each other.

In the late afternoon, I reached the summit of the northern boundary of the park, and then coasted for miles, enjoying an easy descent into the town of Twentynine Palms. (The town's founders could have given the place a simpler name had they planted just one more palm.) This was a military community that served as the Marine Air Ground Task Force Training Command. It reminded me of many of the places I had lived in my youth as the son of a military officer. They all have a similar feel—flags and patriotic decorations, fast cars, loud motorcycles, check cashing stores, fast food restaurants, and young men with sidewall haircuts—but they lack permanence, since most people move every few years to their next assignment. In this respect, I was similar to the town's citizens: just passing through.

A few miles from Twentynine Palms, I reached Lucerne Valley, another small town with a sense of humor; it billed itself a "Town with Character(s)." From there, I headed west on Highway 62, turning into the hot, dry, dusty wind for another 20 miles before arriving in the town of Yucca Valley, where I stopped at the first motel I found, grabbed a quick bite to eat at a dingy Mexican taqueria, and collapsed into bed.

twenty five

Yucca Valley to Victorville, California
Total Ride Mileage: 2,980

I awoke the next morning feeling shaky. At first I thought it was just fatigue, but within minutes of rising, I was sick to my stomach. The only mileage I made that day was between the bed and bathroom. I had little energy even to write in my journal other than this haiku update:

> Feeling sick today
> Knew the taco tasted strange
> Grounded in Yucca

After a day recuperating from food poisoning, I still felt weak, but decided to move out early in the morning to beat the desert heat. As I rode out of Yucca Valley, I was dismayed when I faced an unexpectedly steep, 30-minute long climb immediately after leaving town; however, in hindsight, the word "Valley" in the town's name should have been a clue.

When I finally topped out, I was surrounded by nothing but miles of desert with Joshua trees and little else. In a few places, I passed through small communities with scattered homes, junkyards, feed stores, and the occasional barking dogs—just enough of them to keep my adrenalin flowing. There was no shoulder on the roadway, but traffic was light and the trucks polite, frequently switching lanes to give me room as they passed. Many of them were hauling freshly cut bails of hay, and I grew to enjoy the sweet, moist scent that lingered behind as they passed.

It was an uneventful day of travel and the rhythmic cadence of my pedals freed my mind to wander. Yet, unlike in the past months, eagerness now replaced my constant need for introspection. I was ready to go home.

Reaching Victorville at the end of the day, I turned south on 7th Street, which I discovered was part of historical Route 66, one of the country's original highways, running from Chicago to Los Angeles. After following it for a few miles, I found a motel and checked in at the lobby. The room was small and cramped and facing the highway, but it had a bed, which was all I really cared about. After a shower, I asked the hotel clerk for directions to a place for dinner. He directed me to a rib joint, but it was closed. There was a Mexican restaurant nearby, but after my experience the previous day, my stomach wasn't up to the challenge. Finally, after walking more than a mile, I located a strip mall with an Italian restaurant that advertised "Pasta, Salad, Lasagna and Pizza by the Slice." Perfect, I thought.

The restaurant was empty when I walked up to the counter.

"I'd like a salad please," I said.

"No salad," responded the clerk, a Middle Eastern man with a heavy accent.

"What type of lasagna do you have?"

"No lasagna," he answered without a trace of a smile.

"OK. Tell you what, I'll go with two slices of pizza."

His response? "Only sell medium pizza. No slices."

"Can I get it with tomatoes, olives, and peppers?"

"Only pepperoni."

I looked at him with incredulity and then my stomach won out: "I'd like a medium pepperoni pizza, please".

"Good choice!" he exclaimed and headed back to the kitchen.

I attempted an early start the next morning, but the magnetic force of the Winchell's Donut House shop across the street overpowered me. While enjoying

a glazed and a cup of coffee, I looked at the map and decided to follow former Route 66 through Antelope Valley toward Palmdale. Of course, because
it wasn't marked as Route 66 but rather as a series of different roads, I had to
stop periodically to ask for directions to confirm that I was on the right route.

One of those stops was at an AM/PM mini-mart a few miles beyond
Victorville. I bought a couple of bottles of Gatorade and asked at the counter
whether I was on the correct road. The clerk was uncertain, but a customer
chimed in with what he thought were the right directions to Palmdale. He was
in his mid-twenties, wearing a slouch hat, gold earrings, tight black rayon shirt,
and chewing on a toothpick. He looked a bit like a younger version of Snoop
Dogg.

"Ya goin' there on your bike?"

"Hopefully, depending on the headwinds."

"You the man, homie."

"Not really, I'm just a middle-aged guy trying to lose some weight," I joked.

"Ya goin' ta lose a lot of weight if you ridin' all the way to Palmdale!"

"Actually, I'm riding across the country. I started in Florida a couple of
months ago."

"Whaaat? Whaaat?"

Suddenly, everyone in the store began speaking at once, offering me directions and asking questions. I couldn't keep track of all the routes recommended
or even understand the differences, so after a few minutes I thanked everyone
and took my drinks out to my bike. As I did, the same guy followed and stood
beside me as I was packing the drinks into my panniers.

"Why?" he asked in a plaintive voice with his hands outstretched.

"Why what?" I replied.

"Why ya doin' this?"

"Because I have some time off from work, and I thought it would be a
great chance to get in shape, see the country, and meet people."

He stared at me for a few long moments, slowly shook his head, and walked
to his car without another word. I knew my answer was lacking depth, drama,
and even a convincing rationale, but how else could I explain what I was doing?

twenty six

Victorville to Ventura, California
Total Ride Mileage: 3,113

Leaving Victorville at mid-morning, I traced the edge of the still snow-capped San Bernardino Mountains to the south; to the north, empty tracts of new houses awaited an end to the recession. Faded billboards nearby advertised homes for "No Down Payment" and "EZ Credit," while a newer one promoted "Bankruptcy by Phone." Dust devils and large tumbleweeds blew down the streets and past the vacant houses, porches, garages, and empty yards. It was a Western ghost town for the 21st century.

The quick-moving tumbleweeds also announced the return of my nemesis: the wind. The forecast had promised strong gusts, but I had no idea how forceful they would be. The difficulty with headwind wasn't just inefficiency, although that was a significant issue. The bigger concern was psychological. The relentless sound of the wind drowned out everything and was a form of psychological torture. After a few hours, it became a force of failure. I felt disillusioned, depressed, frustrated, and ready to quit. To ease the stress, I tried to stop wherever I could find shelter—behind a wooden fence, on the leeward side of a parked truck, within a cluster of pine trees on the side of the road. One of the locals, however, evidently saw things differently. Along a stretch of unprotected highway, a large hand-painted sign stood in the middle of the windswept landscape. It said: "The Wind is Our Friend," followed by a happy face.

Near Littlerock, I pulled over at a tourist operation called Charlie Brown Farms and ate a buffalo burger (they also offered beef, venison, turkey, and ostrich) at a picnic table on the enclosed patio and tried to settle my nerves. Exemplifying the finest of American cuisine, I noted that the menu also included deep-fried Oreos, Twinkies, and Snickers, but I decided that with 40 miles of riding still left, an upset stomach would only compound my self-pity.

After lunch, a bit past Palmdale, I pulled over and spoke to a bread deliveryman unloading his van in front of the market. We leaned close to make ourselves heard over the wind as I asked him about the route to Santa Clarita, figuring that he was familiar with the local roads. He suggested that I take the Sierra Highway/Soledad Canyon Road, which turned out to be good advice because I later found out that the highway I had intended to ride didn't permit cyclists.

One advantage of the route he recommended was that Soledad Canyon was deep enough that it was sheltered from the wind. Another was the scenery, which I grew to appreciate as the road curved in a gradual descent along the perimeter of the Angeles National Forest. My mood immediately lightened, and I could finally concentrate on my surroundings. As I coasted long distances, I saw beautiful gated homes and ranches adjacent to properties filled with decades of junk reminiscent of the *Beverly Hillbillies*. There were also expansive private campgrounds with baseball fields, swimming pools, paddleboats, barbecues, and horseshoe and volleyball courts. Yet I didn't see a single person anywhere. It made me feel as if I were in one of those late 1950s science fiction movies in which the protagonist is the last person on earth. At one point, I descended past the Shambala Preserve, an animal sanctuary run by the actress Tippi Hedren. Set against the creek that runs through this area, it appeared to be a large private zoo, with acres of cages and artificial animal habitats. But it also was strangely empty of both animals and humans.

As the road climbed out of the canyon and crossed under Highway 14 toward Santa Clarita, the full force of the wind again slammed me. Pelted by sand and dust, my face received an unrequested dermabrasion. Newspapers, plastic bags, and other trash were blown against my body and into my spokes. I wasn't riding anymore; it was more like barely controlled wobbling. I pedaled for miles before at last I struggled into the town of Santa Clarita, where I found a rundown roadside motel for the night and checked in for the evening.

Sometime during the early morning hours I was startled awake by explosive pounding outside my room, combined with loud, drunken shouting. As my heart accelerated, I threw on my pants, located my glasses, and opened the door, only to get a brief glimpse of a man stomping angrily down the hallway to the hotel exit. The door of the room next to me had been on the receiving end of his fist, and the floor was littered with large fragments of pressboard. I never learned the reason for the man's rage, but as I headed back to my bed, I pledged to start spending more on my future accommodations.

After a fitful few hours of remaining sleep, I packed and rode out into a cool, beautiful morning. The verdant mountains of Canyon Country, as this area was known, were draped with billowing, low-hanging cumulus clouds. Every few moments, mottled blue sky and sunshine attempted to break through. Except for the heavily trafficked four-lane highway, the ride was relaxing and became even more so as the day continued and the temperature warmed. On either side, orchards of orange trees lined the road for miles. Fragrant threads of the season's last orange blossoms filled the air. Along with the scenery, it made for an intoxicating few miles as I rode through the small farming communities of Piru and Fillmore and into Santa Paula.

Leaning my bike against a streetlamp, I took a break to explore Santa Paula and stretch my legs. It was a small, diverse, and vibrant community. In the town park, a statue memorialized the 1928 failure of the St. Francis Dam, an event that resulted in the death of more than 450 people. Gazing at the memorial, I recalled reading about this tragedy in Marc Reisner's excellent book *Cadillac Desert* (which should be required reading for every California citizen). It's one thing to read about an event almost a century past. But to realize the crushing force of the resulting flood that drove 12 billion gallons of water from Santa Clarita to Santa Paula, covering much of the route I had travelled in my hours of riding that day—it was horrific to consider.

After departing from Santa Paula, I turned onto Highway 150 and headed up the climb toward Ojai. It was here that I started to sense that I was finally "home" in Northern California. At a cyclist's pace, I could observe the subtle changes between different life zones. From the window of a car it's all a seamless blur, but, from a leather saddle, these transitions are as distinct as chapters in a book. A few days before, I was riding through the lower Sonoran zone filled with saguaro. This slowly transformed into the Mojave zone of the Joshua tree. And, now, along this windy, bucolic two-lane road, I was increasingly noticing the wild sunflowers, miner's lettuce, valley oak, toyon, and salvia of the California transition zone. I rode toward the summit, enjoying these longtime friends, reminders of home.

One of my companions on the ride was the great author of the West, Wallace Stegner. I carried several of his novels with me and was reading one of them, *Crossing to Safety*, which begins with these opening lines:

> "Floating upward through a confusion of dreams and memory, curving like a trout through the rings of previous risings, I surface. My eyes open. I am awake."

I can find no better description of how I felt as I tried to get out of bed the next morning. For a change, I didn't have to concern myself with scorpions, drunks, or the amorous nocturnal wrestling matches of others. The previous night I was fortunate enough to stay at a friend's vacant vacation home in the small village of Ojai. It was one of those secluded country homes that was so quiet, so peaceful, that it was difficult to rouse myself to consciousness the following morning. It was as if the soft feather bed created an intense gravitational field pulling me into the mattress, and it wasn't until the early afternoon that I could muster the energy to depart.

As I left Ojai, I followed a bicycle path the entire distance to Ventura. It initially curved through scenic, remote valleys and, later, in one section, passed along an abandoned, graffiti-covered oil refinery like something from the Apocalypse or the movie *Mad Max*. The forceful winds from the west heightened the effect: loose aluminum siding slapped against the refinery tanks, metal chains clanked against rusted oil derricks, and strange squeaking sounds emanated from unknown areas.

However, the most memorable part of the day was watching the sandpipers. In part, it was because these are fascinating birds. Sandpipers, which are members of the Scolopacidae family, use the tactile receptors in their bills to forage for food under the sand. I've spent many hours observing how they quickly probe the sand for sustenance while under the constant threat of oncoming surf. On that day, I particularly enjoyed watching them for another reason. It was because their habitat was along the shoreline. It meant that I had finally reached the Pacific Ocean.

Near Ventura, I found an opening in a chain-link fence and squeezed my bike through it and over the Amtrak train tracks and walked down to the beach to dunk my wheels in the Pacific. Then I sat in the sand next to my bike, looking out at the sandpipers and the surf, surprisingly choked with emotion. I had done it. I had traversed the country alone, under my own power—and much of it while wearing Lycra. I had faced off against brutal winds, crappy weather, frightening dogs, mechanical failure, extreme fatigue, homesickness, and even painful chafing. But I made it.

twenty seven

Ventura to San Simeon State Park, California
Total Ride Mileage: 3,358

Although I had crossed the country, I still had miles to go before I was home. Pedaling north toward Ventura, I followed a combination of bike paths and the Pacific Coast Highway through Carpinteria and Montecito and into Santa Barbara. The "PCH" has an almost mythological connotation for most Americans. The winding road is framed by the sand and blue waves of the Pacific and the rocks and green vegetation of the surrounding mountains. It is spectacularly beautiful and brings to mind convertibles and Coppertone, bikinis and board shorts, youth and possibility.

I pedaled the PCH feeling energized, but the wind was as well. To make matters worse, on several occasions a car would pull alongside and the driver would roll down the window to indicate that he wanted to say something. I would be forced to slow down to nearly a standstill so that I could hear over the sound of the wind. Then the driver would inevitably shout something profound like: "Wow, it must be tough riding in this wind."

Late in the afternoon, I pedaled up State Street and into downtown Santa Barbara. To celebrate, I checked into a motel, showered, and found an upscale Japanese restaurant for dinner. I'm sure I looked a bit out of place—a grizzled, middle-aged man sitting alone at a table staring intently at a map, dressed in cargo camping slacks and a black well-worn cycling shirt. I was just thankful that I was left alone, and the waiter was inattentive. Perhaps it was the bottle of sake, maybe it was my frustration battling the wind, or it could have been the realization that my ride was nearing its end and I was almost home, but I was experiencing a tangle of emotions that were very close to the surface.

Before leaving Santa Barbara the following morning, I found a market to replenish my food supplies for my last week of camping. For me this meant pouches of tuna, apples and bananas, fresh tortillas, cheese, an avocado, and my guilty pleasure: a box of frosted blueberry Pop-Tarts. The limited selection of the markets in the South was now a distant memory, and I stuffed my panniers with as much as they would hold.

I followed Highway 1 until reaching the fork to Lompoc and then took the turnoff toward Jalama Beach. Because this is a 14-mile road that terminates at the ocean, it was almost completely free of traffic. The only evidence of humans was the road itself, which ran through a number of beautiful valleys teeming with freshly blooming California golden poppies, along with a few solitary ranches. It was the kind of road of which cyclists dream, with smooth pavement, rolling hills, and views that constantly delighted.

As I approached the beach in the late afternoon, the wind again attempted to hinder my progress. In my mind, it had now replaced the threat of canines, and on some days even a slight breeze was enough to make me anxious. Today it was a strong and constant force, and as I slogged against it, I began to harbor the dark thought that it was not some atmospherically caused flow of air, but a malevolent being attempting to keep me from my family.

I finally reached the campground in a state of thorough exhaustion, checked in at the ranger station, and tried to find a protected campsite, but they were all taken. Instead, I parked my bicycle against a fence and walked over to the restroom area for a shower. The good news was that the campground had warm showers; the bad news was that the stench suggested they should have received Superfund Cleanup status. "Soap, rinse, and retch" was not the most enjoyable way to get clean.

In an attempt to loosen the tightness in my aching legs, I took a walk on the beach—and it was certainly among the most resplendent of the Central Coast—but the wind blistered me with sand and made it impossible to keep my glasses on. There was a local beach café nearby, and I took the opportunity to try one of its famous "Jalama Burgers" as an excuse to sit inside the glass enclosed patio protected from the wind. As I ate, I watched a large number of people packing their campers and RVs and heading away from Mother Nature's onslaught. I wished I had that option, but I was exhausted, and it was getting late.

After the café closed, I walked through the campground, trying to find somewhere sheltered, again without success. Since arriving, I had witnessed a parade of umbrellas, large plastic trash bins, tents, and coolers blowing through the campground like tumbleweeds. This wind was more forceful than any I had faced during the previous months. Finally, I ended up pulling all my belongings into a slightly shielded area in front of the café to await darkness. Huddled, watching the sunset, I nursed my last cache of medicinal agave juice to help keep warm, while I engaged in a mental debate over which had been worse: the dogs of St. Landry Parish, Louisiana, or the zephyr I'd been facing the last 1,000 miles.

After the sun disappeared, I reluctantly left the front of the café and found a depression in the lawn near the children's playground where I could bury myself deep in my sleeping bag. It offered only slight protection and for the first part of the night I felt as if I were in a wind tunnel with the swing set overhead creaking loudly and unceasingly. Then, a few hours before sunrise, the howling wind stopped so abruptly that I awoke. A full moon reflected off the placid ocean; an abundance of stars twinkled overhead. A sense of peace and calm enveloped me, and I drifted back to sleep and didn't awaken until daybreak.

I was getting closer to home now and could almost sense the proximity of my family. As I rode through the vegetable fields of the Central Coast toward Pismo Beach, I began to think of Liz and the children more often, anxious to see their smiles, to hear their laughter, to feel their embrace. When I did, my cadence would quicken.

Pismo Beach was my destination for the night. This California state park uniquely permits people to drive their vehicles onto the sand and camp anywhere. On this day the beach was crowded with families, fraternity parties, and fishermen, and I was worried about camping on the sand and being flattened in the middle of the night by a motor home or 4x4 truck. Fortunately, I found another section of the park that had some secluded campsites located inland from the beach. After unpacking and laying out my tarp and sleeping bag, I carried my food, cooking gear, and stove to a bluff above the beach where I prepared dinner, watched the vehicular chaos below, and enjoyed a life-affirming sunset.

Given my campsite's proximity to the ocean, the dew was dense that night, and my saturated sleeping bag took an hour to dry once the sun rose the following morning. But, I didn't mind the delay. I had Mr. Stegner for company and was in no rush to leave, since the day's destination, San Luis Obispo, was less than a few hours' ride. The only interruption in my peaceful morning was a large gaggle of geese eating insects near my campsite table. There were so many that I grabbed my camera for a photograph, disregarding my pledge to take animal photographs only from a distance. When I was within five feet of them, a large white goose sounded the clarion, and suddenly I had six geese aggressively chasing me through the campground until I jumped up on the picnic table for protection. First dogs. Now geese. What's next? I wondered.

It was early afternoon when I reached San Luis Obispo, a town I hadn't visited for nearly 30 years. Not much had changed. It was still very much a college community with a culture reflected in the acronym by which it is affectionately called: "SLO." As I pedaled onto Higuera Street, there was no "Welcome to San Luis Obispo, Heart of the Galaxy, Most Important City on Earth" chest-beating type of sign that you see in many towns trying to promote their communities. Instead, it merely said, "City Limits," as if the residents felt that understatement better conveyed who they were. After I checked into a motel and completed the chores of washing my clothes and cleaning my bike, I explored the downtown area, which was largely as I remembered it—intimate, unhurried, and friendly.

The thing that tells you everything about San Luis Obispo is Bubble Gum Alley, which contains what is possibly the largest collection of DNA outside of the FBI headquarters in Washington, D.C. For decades, people had been turning the corner down this alley off Higuera and Marsh streets, removing the chewing gum from their mouths, and placing it on the brick walls like multicolored pebbles. I remembered the alley from a visit when I was in college, and it was still there. At times in the past, the city government would periodically strip the walls with high-pressure water hoses, but eventually they decided to take a more relaxed attitude and to just let it be. That relaxed attitude reflected the spirit of San Luis Obispo.

The next morning I rode toward Los Osos and then Morro Bay. It was a day of cycling that I like to refer to as a "Mortgage Ride." Yes, the housing prices in California are ridiculously high when compared to the rest of the nation. However, on a day like that, I would have happily made any mortgage payment. As I rode through Los Osos Valley, small pockets of morning fog resembled curtains gradually drawn back to reveal a stunningly beautiful countryside. The hills, marshes, and wetlands were a green-hued canvas to old red barns, purple thistles, multi-colored sweet pea, red-winged blackbirds, and chestnut-colored cows. There was not a cloud in the sky, nor, thankfully, any wind.

Hell, I would have made two payments that day.

I had travelled that portion of Highway 1 dozens of times by car during my life. Always in a rush to get from the northern or southern reaches of the state, I'd never stopped to explore what was around me. I realized this while enjoying a cup of coffee and watching the surfers down by the pier in Cayucos, a small oceanside village where I stopped for a late breakfast. How could I never have visited this place? It was a wonderful, laid-back beach community with a number of funky shops and places to eat. As I soaked in the sunshine with coffee in hand, I wondered how much of life I had missed by being focused on where I was going rather than what I was experiencing.

A few miles out of Cayucos, I saw a cyclist on a racing bike heading south. I gave him a quick wave and was surprised a few moments later when he made a U-turn across the highway and caught up with me. Scott was from Seattle. He was a graphic artist who had previously managed a bicycle shop. He was visiting his sister who lived in the area and, given the blissful weather and scenery, had decided to get out for a Mortgage Ride as well. As he pedaled alongside me, he shared interesting stories of a ride he had made between Alaska and San Diego a few years earlier with a girlfriend. While on that trip, Scott had met another cyclist who had planned his entire route to end each night at a micro-brewery or at the house of someone who was a member of a home brew club. On some days, this strategy had necessitated covering extremely long distances, but the rider felt that the hops and barley were a fitting reward for the extra effort. My kind of cyclist, I thought, and I immediately stored that idea away for a future trip.

Minutes after leaving Scott, I met another cyclist, this one a touring rider heading south. He was dressed in a multicolored T-shirt and board shorts with a bicycle that was overloaded with gear held in place by an intricate web of rope, bungee cords, and straps. His name was Ira, and although he proclaimed himself to be "just a city boy" and a neophyte to both camping and touring, he was going for it in a big way.

Just out of college, Ira had started riding in Vancouver and was on his way to San Diego. But this was a warm-up. From there he was planning to fly to Amsterdam and cycle to Istanbul. He was in a state somewhere between euphoria and delirium as he described his experiences to date—getting lost, enduring hail and rain, and battling a variety of mechanical issues. Most tiring of all, however, were the repeated phone calls he received from his very worried mother. Yet, through it all, Ira was undaunted and committed to pursing his adventure.

In the late afternoon I decided to stop at San Simeon State Park, a few miles south of Hearst Castle, to camp for the night. After unpacking, I walked down to the beach and found a secluded spot where I stripped off my cycling clothes and took a brisk swim in the ocean. As I floated in the rolling waves, I marveled at the beauty of the setting sun on the Big Sur coastline. It had to be one of the most striking landscapes on the planet. From my vantage point, floating in the water, I looked up and down the coast seeing no evidence of man. It was as if I was an explorer from the past discovering a new world.

When I finally left the water and dried off, it was twilight, and I was numb to the marrow and pruned like an apple doll. I walked back to the campsite in a state of chilled bliss. Passing a neighboring site, a fellow camper called out to ask if I would like to join him by the fire and enjoy some wine. Clearly some benevolent cycling god was looking after me.

Erwin was from Holland. Handsome, gregarious, and engaging, he was on his fourth trip to the United States, all of them spent exploring the western part of the country. As we threw back our wine and opened a second bottle, he recounted his wanderings through Utah, Wyoming, Oregon, and California.

"Americans are so different than Europeans," he said.

"How so?"

"Europeans have airs. Everyone is focused on having the right appearance, acting the right way. Your countrymen are open and independent and never seem to care what anyone else thinks. And the western part of America is just like I imagined it as a boy."

I listened for several more minutes as Erwin described with excitement all the places he travelled in the West. I'm always impressed at how people from other countries, and especially those from Europe, have visited more of the United States than many of our citizens. Hearing the passion in Erwin's voice as he described all that he had seen and experienced was a reminder of why, to much of the world, "America" is as much an idea as it is a physical place. It was a feeling that had been rekindled in me over the past 3,000 miles.

twenty eight

San Simeon State Park, California, to…home.
Total Ride Mileage: 3,560

Mortgage Ride one day. Misery Ride the next.

It might have been the wine, or maybe it was just fatigue, but I slept well that night. Perhaps a little too well. I awoke to the chatter of a half dozen crows perched on various parts of my bicycle. As I groggily opened my eyes, I noticed that they were pecking at trash scattered around my sleeping bag. Thinking that the wind had overturned a trash can, I arose and started collecting the litter. That's when I finally noticed that it was my food. Judging by the muddy paw prints on my panniers, it looked as if a number of raccoons had raided my pantry. They had stealthily unzipped four of the pockets on my panniers as I slept and stripped me of every single bit of food. Although I was sleeping next to my bicycle, I never heard a thing.

After cleaning the mess, I packed and headed out in the direction of Big Sur, stopping in San Simeon to eat breakfast and resupply. This portion of Highway 1 has one of the most dramatic and scenic coastlines in the country. However, most of what I saw that day was my front wheel as I tried to keep my head down in the face of cold, hammering winds from the north. On occasion, the leeward side of a mountain would offer protection, but as soon as I rounded the corner, the full blast of the wind would hit me, sometimes shoving me in the direction of oncoming cars.

I stopped a few times to catch my breath and enjoy the scenery: the spectacular mountains of the Ventana Wilderness, the white-capped chop of the Pacific, the molting elephant seals lounging on the sand. But these pauses were brief because I found that I could stay warm only while pedaling. A number of other cyclists headed south, reveling in their amazing tailwind. Most of them gave me a quick wave and an empathetic grin, but given the conditions, no one stopped to talk.

The highway climbed precipitously along the face of the mountains until I was pedaling on the face of the cliffs more than 1,500 feet above the ocean. Long stretches of the road were under construction. Most likely, this roadwork was due to the heavy rains from earlier in the winter, since there were still rivulets of water and mud running down the hillside. In some areas, I had the uneasy feeling that the cliffs above me could break free at any time. I navigated them with an open eye until I reached my campsite in Pfeiffer Big Sur State Park in the early evening. By then I was so chilled that I parked my bike, grabbed a change of clothes, and went immediately into a hot shower. Once I was warm, I returned to my campsite and ate some freeze-dried pasta and then crawled into my bag, feeling thoroughly exhausted.

First, however, I bagged my food and hung it from a tree. The raccoons would need to find their own meal that night.

The following day, the wind lessened, permitting me to enjoy the countryside in this area of Big Sur. At times, I felt as if I were riding through *Christina's World,* the famous painting by Andrew Wyeth with its long, flowing grasses and worn wooden buildings. While I was stopped at an overlook enjoying the view, a southbound touring cyclist pulled over to my side of the road. Jack was from Canada. Even if he hadn't mentioned it, I would have known it by his modest, friendly demeanor and the occasional "eh?" and "a boot" in his speech. At the age of 47, he had pulled the plug and quit his career as an Air Force officer, sold his possessions, and was now riding from British Columbia to the tip of South America. His bike was rigged with a precision reflecting a career in the military. Mounted on his handlebars was a variety of high-tech gadgetry, including a GPS, camera, high-intensity light, electric horn, and mobile phone.

In much of life, when initially introduced to a stranger, such as at work or a cocktail party, it takes time to break the ice and form even a temporary relationship. However, I found that when I met other touring cyclists this process was significantly shortened since I already knew that we shared many experiences, personal goals, and sore muscles. Thus, in the space of a few minutes, it was easy to develop a bond with someone, as I did with Jack. But the road also ensures that these interludes are brief. Jack and I were headed in opposite directions, each with miles to go. So, after a few minutes of conversation, we exchanged contact information, shook hands, and departed our separate ways.

That afternoon, I rode through Carmel, Monterey, and Seaside. I didn't have a detailed map, and cyclists were prohibited on this stretch of Highway 1, so I generally just headed north on surface streets, bouncing around like a ball in a Pachinko machine until I ended my day in a motel in Marina where I checked in, unloaded my gear, and jumped into the shower.

As I was drying off there was a knock on the door. It was my brothers, Kevin and Doug, who had driven the two hours from home to take me out to dinner.

"Seriously? You ride across the country and you still have a gut? How is that possible?" Kevin said as he forced his way through the door slapping my stomach.

"Mike, I don't know if it's the gear, your clothes, or you, but something really reeks in here," added Doug pushing in behind him.

Over dinner, the teasing subsided. After we had caught up on family and friends and they had finished peppering me with questions, Kevin looked across the table at me: "I can't believe you're almost home. You're really going to make it." For most of our lives the Dillon brothers had been inseparable friends. Aside from this trip or when one of us was away at college, we had always been together. Seeing them again overwhelmed me with thoughts of home and I returned to my motel room unable to sleep as I tossed with excitement.

Pedaling through the sleepy fishing village of Moss Landing the following day, I could feel my mood rising. Nearby Elkhorn Slough was one of my favorite places for bird-watching and kayaking, and it was only a short drive from my home. For the remainder of the day, I relaxed and rode at a leisurely pace, winding through the farming communities of Watsonville, Freedom, Aptos, and into Santa Cruz, lost in thought as I tried to commit to memory the final moments of my ride. It was a spectacular day along the famous Santa Cruz

Boardwalk with the crisp, cool seasonal temperature beginning to give way to the intense sunlight of the cloudless skies. In the early-season tourists sitting bundled on the beach, I could sense the promise of summer just a few weeks away.

Tomorrow, I thought, I would finally be home. I wondered how my body would react when I applied the brakes one last time. My legs had become almost separate sentient beings. They seemed to anticipate and embrace the daily distances. Over the previous months, my morning commute had changed from drinking coffee from a travel mug while creeping along in highway traffic, to pedaling 20 or 30 miles before breakfast. Often I would travel for hours, distracted in thought and by my surroundings, unconsciously spinning my pedals.

I went to sleep that evening with visions of reuniting with family and friends, of sharing my experiences, of hearing stories of all that I had missed. But these warm thoughts were rapidly replaced by other less welcome prospects: finding a new job, awakening to an alarm clock (instead of a wild turkey), and the normal responsibilities of life.

"Re-entry" was going to be tough. Very tough.

I awoke with first light, packed quietly, and slipped out, trying not to wake the friends who were serving as my hosts for the night. Riding through the streets of Santa Cruz in the misty, early dawn, I shared the morning with only gulls and a few surf-casting fishermen in hooded sweatshirts.

As the sun rose, I met a good friend at a local diner called Zachary's where I enjoyed one last high-calorie breakfast and caught up with him over a pot of hot coffee. I like to call him "Astro Boy," not only for his striking resemblance to that character of Japanese manga and early 1960s American cartoons, but also because of his strength as a rider. He was an accomplished cyclist who had raced semi-professionally for nearly a decade and who rode at such a level that his shaved legs were not cause for ridicule. Astro Boy had offered to keep me company as I headed on the final part of my journey over the Santa Cruz Mountains to home.

We started out through downtown Santa Cruz and up Highway 9 into the cool, moist redwood forests surrounding the former logging towns of Felton and Ben Lomond. As I climbed the 20 miles to the top of the mountain, I reflected on everything I'd experienced over the previous months. Unfortunately, those memories were becoming individual ingredients in a thoroughly blended neural soup. I found that I couldn't recall whether I had spoken to that interesting ranch hand in Navasota, Texas, or Blythe, California. I wasn't sure if that wondrously desolate desert road had been in Peridot, Arizona, or outside of Hatch, New Mexico. The young woman who told me about the challenges of raising her daughter in a small southern town: Had that been in Gulfport or Bay St. Louis, Mississippi? Where was it that Don had first regaled me with an evening of his tales? The ingredients were blending, and, increasingly, all I was left with was the overall taste, or "sabor," of the experience.

At the summit of the climb, Astro Boy and I paused to add a layer of clothing to keep warm on the steep descent toward home. He encouraged me to lead, making excuses as to why I would be faster, given the weight of my bicycle and gear. I knew, however, that this gesture was because he understood that I needed some distance not for the weight I was carrying, but for the emotion I was bearing. My thoughts and feelings were a bubbling caldron. I was almost home. Almost done. Yet something in me didn't want to stop riding. As much as I felt the pull of family, another part of me wanted to turn east and continue in motion.

I flew down the hill with rapturous abandon. My bike, my legs, my heart, and the road became one, and I descended at speed, almost without notice of anything but the pavement ahead. At the bottom of the hill, my eyes suddenly began to water, not from the wind, but because there on the side of the road were my father and youngest son, Bryce, seated on their bicycles, waiting to greet me. It was completely unexpected, and as I skidded to a stop, we hugged, and I saw tears in my father's eyes as well. Bryce wrapped his arms around my waist and began talking at a machine gun-like pace, as if to tell me in the space of a single breath everything I had missed. After a few moments of reunion, I found myself ready to get moving and we rode off together—three generations on our bicycles.

A few miles later, I made my last climb of the ride. This one was on the road to my house. Without my realizing it, the others fell back, and as I climbed

I was surprised by dozens of friends, family, and colleagues who had lined the road holding cardboard signs and were clapping and ringing bells to welcome me home. I was stunned and overcome with emotion as I turned into my driveway, brought my bicycle to a final stop, and wrapped my arms around Liz.

twenty nine

A Closing Thought

When I decided to make this ride and began speaking about it with others, I encountered what a close friend used to refer to as "The Wall of No." Almost everyone had a reason why I shouldn't do it:

"What if you get robbed?"

"What if you have an accident?"

"You're not in shape; you'll have a heart attack."

"You might get lost."

"Your bicycle could break."

None of these things occurred—or came close to occurring. Instead, almost every encounter was positive. From Lori, the waitress I met in Jacksonville to Erwin, a fellow traveler from Holland, and the dozens of others that I haven't written about, people were overwhelming friendly, supportive, and helpful.

Early in the trip, while riding through St. Landry Parish in Louisiana, I had a conversation with a man leaving a convenience store. He asked where I was going and whether there had been any problems in St. Landry. I told him I was headed to Acadia Parish and that everything had been wonderful. He proudly responded, "Good. You'll be fine here. Folks will look after you. Nice people here. You have nothin' to worry about. But you need to watch you'self when you get to Acadia. It's mighty dangerous there. Be careful!"

I thanked him for the advice and a day later rode into Acadia Parish. As I was standing in front of a small market, a man walked over to me and struck up a conversation about my trip. When I told him that I had just traveled through

St. Landry Parish, he exclaimed incredulously, "You didn't get robbed there? Nothing happened? Boy, you was lucky. St. Landry is one dangerous place."

The point of this story is that American used to be the "home of the brave." Now, I'm not so sure. What struck me as I travelled through the country is how as individuals and as a country we have become fragmented and fearful. Perhaps this is in reaction to the horrific events of 9/11, the War on Terrorism, and the recession. Certainly, the era of Nancy Grace-style media coverage only makes things worse. All I know is that this is not how or who we used to be.

What I found is that if you give in to fear, you will never see that amazing field of purple lupine on that lonely dirt road. You won't enjoy the camaraderie of a fellow traveler and have it develop into a friendship. You won't stand in the middle of an expanse of desert at dawn and enjoy almost perfect silence and solitude. You won't experience the soft, loving voice of an elderly woman in a small bayou town who holds your hands and prays for your safety.

If I learned anything from my ride, it is that when we let fear limit us, we miss the best of each other, our country, and ourselves. So, be not afraid.

But do keep an eye out for the dogs.

thirty

Epilogue

I think often about my time riding across the country. Sometimes it happens when I open the newspaper. That was the case in late April 2010, when I saw a photograph in the *New York Times* of citizens of Bayou La Batre and read about the devastating impact of the Deepwater Horizon oil spill on the town and surrounding areas. Although I had spent only two days in this Louisiana bayou fishing village, it was enough to connect me to the personal, economic, and environmental dimensions of this disaster. To me, it was more than just a story in the newspaper.

Sometimes I call to mind memories of the ride in the middle of a stress-packed day of meetings at work or while crawling along the highway with thousands of other morning commuters. When I do, I remember the sense of freedom I felt riding alone through remote stretches of our country, as well as my appreciation for its people and cultural diversity. I also value the sense of perspective I gained.

But, mostly, I think of the friendships I formed with other cyclists.

I first encountered Jan and Irene in DeRidder, Texas. They were two grand-mothers from Michigan who enjoyed adventure and quilting. I thought of them as who Thelma and Louise would have become a later in life had they not driven over that cliff. When Jan decided to ride her beloved bike "Esmerelda" across the country, her friend Irene provided companionship and a van for SAG support. After 116 days, Jan completed her ride. Not far from Ocean Park, California, she pedaled up "the last mountain I EVER intend to climb!" and descended a few minutes later to the Pacific Ocean near San Diego.

Two years later, at the age of 64, she decided that she needed to see if she could do a long ride without any support. Over the course of three weeks, she rode successfully from Evansville, Indiana, to Lansing, Michigan, with only Esmerelda and her basket of stuffed animals for company.

Larry was a city planner from Seattle who had lost his job as a result of recession downsizing. He had planned to use his forced time off for, as he described it, a "U-shaped" crossing of the country beginning from his home, heading down the coast to San Diego, across the southern U.S., and up the East Coast. We crossed paths in a campground near Fort Davis, Texas, where we shared a meal and a bottle of wine, seated at a campground picnic bench under a star-filled Texas sky. After 6,200 miles, Larry completed his ride in Chautauqua, New York.

Don finished his journey in San Diego and then returned to his cabin in a remote part of Alaska, where he lives for much of the year. But his wanderlust continued. Over the next few years, I received dozens of emails from him, regaling me with stories of crossing the country again, this time while driving a truck and towing a storage container he had converted into his MBC (Mobile Base Camp); working construction in Dutch Harbor in the Aleutian Islands; and accompanying his girlfriend on another cycling adventure, this one a 30-day ride through Alaska and into Canada.

I always knew that Don and I would reconnect and, in 2012, we did. My youngest son and I and a few friends traveled to Alaska for an extended kayak trip in Prince William Sound. When we arrived to pick up our gear in Valdez, Don was waiting to meet us. He was departing the next morning on a multi-month construction job in one of the remote fisheries in the Sound, but we enjoyed a wonderful evening together, and I had the pleasure of introducing my son to this unique character who added so much color to an interesting chapter in my life.

I haven't seen Don since then, but we are still in close touch. His latest idea is for me to quit my job and join him on an extended ride across Tasmania.

It did take me a bit of time to re-enter the "real world," and it was a few weeks before I felt fully integrated into the pace and daily responsibilities of family and home. A few months after I returned, I rejoined the corporate labor force and now work for a large public software company where I do, on occasion, look out the window and contemplate the next place I want to ride.

People often ask me about my trip and how it changed me. When they do, I usually find myself at a loss, stumbling to find a way of articulating what I learned from the experience. So let me leave it as this:

It's never too late to change your cadence and enjoy a little adventure.

January 2014

Acknowledgments

This book originated from a blog I kept as I crossed the country. Through word-of-mouth, readership grew and many readers suggested that I write a book about my experience. Without their encouragement, I don't think the thought of a book would ever have occurred to me. I have changed some names in the interest of individuals' privacy. The dialogue has been recreated from my notes and recollections.

Before I returned to the workforce, I put together a draft of this book and asked Jill Patton, a journalist I know, if she would take a look at it. She did, and in the kindest way possible told me (in essence), "This is a piece of crap." But she also persuaded me that there was something there if I wanted to keep working on it. She explained that most writers go through 50 or 60 drafts before they get close to having something to publish. In retrospect, she was about right. Jill, thank you for the initial encouragement.

A neighbor referred me to Marisa Milanese for assistance with editing. Although I have never met her in person since she lives on the opposite side of the country, Marisa was a wonderful help in making revisions and persuading me to push on when I questioned whether it was worth the effort.

I had additional editorial support from Steve Karp, Jacob Garber, Emily Dillon, Jennifer Rubalcava, Gary Kissiah and Sharon Smith who read the manuscript and provided comments. A big note of gratitude to each of you.

Thanks also to Kevin Story, a friend and accomplished artist, who designed the cover art. You can contact him at kevstory@me.com.

"Mallet" (formerly "The Hammer"), "Pedro," Ricky, Stewart, "Polish Super Hero," "Ho," "T-Dawg," Mark ("Gman"), Karp, Kevin, and Doug—thank you for traveling with me vicariously. But you all are truly bastards for traveling with me only vicariously.

Don, what can I say but "Semper Fi"?

Mom and Dad, as life-long friends, parents and role models, no one could ask for more.

Liz (aka "Wife Command Central"), I don't tell you frequently enough how much your love and support have meant to me through the years. So, now it's here in writing.

Lastly, to Declan, Emily, and Bryce, you remain the most wonderful adventure of my life.

All proceeds from this book will be donated to the Aldar Academy, a non-profit educational institution that does wonderful work helping children and young adults with severe learning and emotional problems. More information can be found at: http://www.aldaracademy.org/.

10213793R00118

Made in the USA
San Bernardino, CA
09 April 2014